BUD

BUD

The Other Side of the Glacier

Bill McGrane

1817

HARPER & ROW, PUBLISHERS, New York
Cambridge, Philadelphia, San Francisco, London
Mexico City, São Paulo, Singapore, Sydney

FIRST EDITION

Designer: Jénine Holmes

Library of Congress Cataloging-in-Publication Data

McGrane, Bill.
    Bud, the other side of the glacier.

    1. Grant, Bud.   2. Football—United States—Coaches—Biography.
3. Minnesota Vikings (Football team)
I. Title.
GV939.G72M38   1986   796.332′092′4 [B]   85-45646
ISBN 0-06-015583-3

86 87 88 89 90 RRD 10 9 8 7 6 5 4 3 2 1

To Harry Grant, Sr.,
and Bert McGrane

Contents

Foreword

There are two Bud Grants, and this story is about both of them.

There is, first, that glacial, unyielding sideline presence.

Used to be a country song . . . it had a line something like ". . . if you want to keep the beer cold, boys, just set it next to my ex-wife's heart. . . ."

Or Bud Grant's stare.

You've probably seen that side of him.

"I didn't know if I should interview him or ski him" was the way one writer put it. Writers have been taking their best cuts at that side of Grant for a long time, which figures, because that's the side most of them see.

I've not seen a skilled surgeon at his work, but I imagine his approach would be quite a bit like that of Grant, the coach.

Dispassionate. Bud felt emotion was a luxury he couldn't afford during a game.

Thorough. He didn't like loose ends at all.

Observant. He studied during a game and not just the high-tech ebb and flow of strategy and tactic. Much of what Grant sought and found was written on the faces and in the body language of players, his and theirs.

Confident. Bud Grant is comfortable being himself.

Entering the 1985 National Football League season, professional teams of his authorship had won 283 games. As a professional coach, he has won more games than Tom Landry or Vince Lombardi or Don Shula or even the legendary Paul Brown. He's never been anything but a player or a head coach. Winnipeg of the Canadian Football League hired him as head coach when he was twenty-nine years old.

He recalls the occasion of being appointed at Winnipeg clearly, because it was the day his father died.

You get that in conversation with Grant . . . a lot of lean and very little fat. He is direct. Not offensive, not really even blunt, and not outspoken.

Direct.

If you elect to take offense, that's your business. If you judge him to be cold or aloof, that is your choice, and he would be the last to question it.

If the truth be told, most of us are not all that confident or comfortable in being ourselves . . . we spend a lot of time and energy in trying to appear as we think others would like for us to appear.

That is not Grant's way.

In a business where histrionics are not only accepted but encouraged, he stood his sideline ground as impassively as the hard north country that reared him.

For Bud Grant, opponents were not to be feared or despised or even disliked. They were problems to be solved. If you are lost in the woods, it does no good to hate the woods . . . better that you use your wits and your knowledge and the courage of your convictions to find your way out of the woods.

That's the public side. . . .

There is the other side of the glacier, too.

"When he started kindergarten," his mother recalled, "the teacher asked me if I was sending Bud to school on time. I said, 'Of course I am, why do you ask?' She said she asked because he was late every morning." So the kindergarten teacher waited along the route to investigate.

"Bud would stop along the way," Bernice Grant said. "He'd get to watching a bird or a bug on the leaf of a tree, and he'd forget about school."

His cousin, Bob Facette, talked him into trying sports when he was a boy.

"It seemed like coaches saw something special in him, right from the start," said Bud's mother.

Sport is two-faced, really . . . be average, and it's fun, but be very bad or very good, and it isn't the same.

"I can remember my nephew [Facette] coming to me and saying, 'Aunt Bernie, it's not fair . . . Bud's our best player, but he gets bawled out more than any of the rest of us,'" said Mrs. Grant.

He quit coaching and then went back to it, which, in the thoughtful words of Cecil Johnson, can be like wearing a pork chop suit into a lion cage.

"When you make a decision," said Grant, "you gather facts and then you weigh them. Everything's a risk if you want to look at it that way . . . or you can flip it over and say that everything is an opportunity. It's up to you to decide."

In June of 1944, Bill Stewart of the Superior, Wisconsin, *Evening Telegram* wrote in his column:

> Harry Grant, Jr., is an all-around athlete, has just turned 17 years old, weighs 205 pounds and is six foot three. He is definitely a natural . . . unlike most big, raw-boned boys of his age, Grant has perfect physical coordination. He is cool and deliberate under fire, whether he is in a tight spot on the gridiron, basketball court, or baseball diamond. His character is of the best, his temperament excellent. In other words, he has all the qualifications of a really great athlete. . . .

Bernice Grant's tone was rather wistful.

"Sport took over his life, it seemed, and it just sort of happened. I remember the rest of us would have supper together, but Bud's plate would be on the back of the stove, warming."

Has she been surprised by her son's success?

"I don't think that much about it," she confessed. "I know he's worked very hard. I'm more pleased at the sort of person he is. All I ever wanted was for Bud to be a person of principle and to be honest at all times. I think he's done that."

He is fond of sweets, delights in pulling off extravagant practical jokes, is a fairly stern father and a total cupcake of a grandfather.

He is comfortable being silent for long periods of time, and when he does speak, it is only after deliberation. He is a lot like those wild creatures he's so fond of . . . light-footed and wary in his appraisal of the bait, no matter how deftly offered.

If you have only seen him as Bud the coach, then you have only seen him when he wears a cap.

He looks different without the cap. There is a hint, especially in profile . . . something in the line of his forehead and the eyes . . . of a stalking cat.

Observant. Not intended for confinement. A leopard, maybe . . . are there gray leopards?

There are.

His success as coach was the gingerbread of his life . . . the meat and potatoes is his belief in himself, his ability to perceive others as they really are, and his even-handed manner in dealing with both of those puzzling constituents.

If you know something of the disease of alcoholism, then you may have heard the "Serenity Prayer."

"God grant me the serenity to accept the things I cannot change, the courage to change the things I can, and the wisdom to know the difference."

I don't know if Bud's ever heard the prayer, but he lives by it.

BUD

1

Over and Back

Paul Krause, the safetyman, said he couldn't remember attending a "nicer affair."

Krause has a beard now and business interests, but his eighty-one career pass interceptions remain a National Football League record, and he made fifty-three of those wearing Viking purple. The nice affair was a dinner honoring the Twenty-Five Year Viking team, the men judged to be the best of the hundreds who had played for the Minnesota franchise since its birth in 1961.

The dinner was held on September 7, 1985, and Paul Krause was an honoree.

So was Mick Tingelhoff, who played center for seventeen years and 240 consecutive games.

Mick saw the tears and understood them.

Bud Grant was to speak for ten minutes, but sat down after little more than two. His audience included not only fans and members of Viking teams past but the 1985 team as well. That team would open the season the following day against the Super Bowl champion San Francisco 49ers.

Grant welcomed the Twenty-Five Year team and saluted its members for their accomplishments. And then he spoke to the young men of his 1985 squad.

"If I could do one thing," said Grant, "I would give the hearts of these men to our present players." His voice wavered after that, and there were tears on his cheeks. And then he sat down.

Fran Tarkenton, the quarterback, was another Twenty-Five Year honoree. Of Grant, Tarkenton said: "When he opens his mouth to speak, he makes more sense than any human being I know of."

Grant spoke to his team the next day, before it took the field against the 49ers. The 1985 49ers appeared, if anything, to be better than the team that had routed Miami in Super Bowl XIX. For their

1

part, the Vikings were essentially the same people who had endured the 3–13 mortification of 1984.

But there was one difference . . . Bud was back.

He told his players not to be discouraged if the 49ers gained a lot of yards . . . the 49ers, he pointed out, gained a lot of yards every week. Try to stay close, Grant counseled, take advantage of mistakes, and try to be there at the end.

In the first half, the 49ers gained 208 yards to the Vikings' 74, but the score was just 7–0 San Francisco, and that touchdown came after a Minnesota fumble on the second play of the game.

Grant spoke to his team again at halftime.

Good teams like the 49ers, he noted, are not accustomed to playing hard for an entire game. Only the poorer teams are accustomed to that, Grant said. Good teams are used to playing hard for two or three quarters and then having the game in hand. Good teams, he concluded, can become frustrated if things aren't going their way. Stay close, Grant urged, and you will have an opportunity to win.

The Vikings stayed close. While a furious Minnesota defense encouraged fumble recoveries and pass interceptions, quarterback Tommy Kramer marched the Vikings to one touchdown and passed for another. When Scott Studwell hit Wendell Tyler with a thunderclap tackle to cause yet another fumble, Doug Martin, a defensive lineman, grabbed the loose ball and ran it to the 49er 1 to arrange another score, and with 2:56 remaining, Minnesota had pulled even at 21-all.

On the sideline, Grant grinned at Jan Stenerud, his golden-age place kicker.

"You sure you can see that far?" he asked. "Can you read jersey numbers that far away?"

Grant referred to a point he had made throughout the week with Stenerud, to kick off to Derrick Harmon and not to Dana McLemore, one of the league's best returnmen.

"Keep kicking to that Number 24," Grant counseled, "he might cough one up."

Stenerud kicked to Harmon at the goal line, which was 29 yards from the spot where Harmon "coughed one up" after Willie Teal's crashing tackle. Joey Browner recovered for the Vikings.

"He has so much common sense," said Stenerud of Grant. "Most of us have common sense the next day . . . Bud has it before a thing happens."

Minnesota won the game . . . Ted Brown, a pouty running back, glanced off tackle for 10 yards and a touchdown and a 28–21 lead. Joe Montana's desperate effort to pull the game out ended with 14 seconds to play when Rufus Bess intercepted for Minnesota in the end zone.

Spectator Tarkenton gave his impressions of the game:

"I sat there thinkin', Am I goin' nuts, or what? Here's this San Francisco team that's really super, but every time they get something goin', there's either a fumble or Montana gets intercepted. Then, I remembered . . . hey, Bud's been winnin' like this for a lot of years."

Afterward, Grant faced the reporters.

"We had tenacity," he said. "Tenacity is something that can be maintained so long as you are rewarded for it. If you're having success, even when you're tired, it's easy to remain tenacious."

A year earlier, Bud Grant had retired as coach of the Minnesota Vikings. On September 2, 1984, the Vikings had opened the season against San Diego, and the day had been marked as a statewide farewell to Grant. In pregame ceremonies, Grant was the recipient of a lot of fancy words and nice gifts. And then the Vikings went out and had the stuffing knocked out of them by the Chargers to launch the year without Bud.

A year later, after he had returned to the job and won the victory over San Francisco, a weary, wild-eyed band of Vikings held a private ceremony for Grant and presented him with a far more meaningful gift . . . the game ball.

As the locker room crowd at last began to dwindle after the win over the 49ers, a veteran football writer approached Grant for a second time. He'd been in the general interview, but his notes troubled him . . . specifically, his lack of notes.

"Come on, Bud," he said, "what are you really feeling? This has to be a fantastic moment for you. Can't you tell me what beating the 49ers really means to Bud Grant?"

He shrugged.

"One win . . . it means one win. It means we've got a long way to go."

It also meant that the man some pundits call Horseshoe Harry had returned.

And the game was the better for it.

Our game is littered with bright, intense, motivated, sophisticated coaches. Out somewhere on the edge of that fiercely striving company, Bud Grant just sort of moseys along . . . observant, comfortable within himself, weighing and measuring so truly.

Is he a great coach?

"I don't know that Bud could diagram five plays," said Fran Tarkenton, without the least bit of rancor. "But, my goodness, does he know people! He excels at managing people and making people decisions. Everybody who plays for Bud understands him . . . he is where the buck stops. There's no committee, there's just Bud."

When the Vikings defeated the 49ers to open the 1985 season,

Bud Grant coached the first game of his second career ... if you want to be picky about it. He spent the 1984 National Football League season under the nameplate-defying title of "Executive Consultant for Organizational Development."

What it meant was that he remained under contract for a year after resigning as coach.

In his "first" career, he coached 457 professional football games, exclusive of exhibitions, over a twenty-seven year span. His teams won 283 games, lost 166, and tied 8. Over that span, teams he coached won a total of 25 assorted championships. Only the late George Halas, with 326 career coaching victories, has won more games than Grant. Bud's ten-year record at Winnipeg in the Canadian League was 122–66–3 and four Grey Cup championships, the CFL Super Bowl.

His seventeen-year record at Minnesota, prior to 1984, was 161–100–5. Ironically, he may be best-known as the coach who got beat every time he went to the Super Bowl, which may be like complaining to the waiter when your steak's fine but the parsley garni is wilted.

His abrupt resignation in 1984 resounded across Minnesota like a sonic boom.

His decision to return impacted equally ... a Metrodome banner early in the 1985 season spoke for most Minnesotans: "Thank God for Bud Grant." In the land of Paul Bunyan, he is truly larger than life.

Most coaching retirements are the by-product of a conversation between the coach and a high-management type. In these conversations, retirement is presented as an attractive option ... the other option is getting fired.

Retirees of this persuasion make vague but high-toned references to the best interests of themselves, their families, and their organization.

Grant just quit.

For two reasons, it would seem. The first is his remarkably clear-eyed understanding of the nature of the job. The second was the fact that his "sums" came out right.

Understanding the job?

"Being a coach ... I can't say it's unique, but it's different than most jobs I know of. The thing in the back of your mind, always, is the insecurity. You have to recognize that your career can be over quickly."

Grant has always seemed about as insecure as a mature oak tree ... but it is a clear-eyed oak tree.

"You can be a victim of things," he explained, "not all of them of your own doing. If key players get hurt, you can't really overcome their loss. And sometimes, things just don't go right . . . you have a run of just plain bad luck. Maybe there's a change in the people who run your club. What if a new man comes in and says, 'We know you've done a good job here, but you understand . . . we'd be more comfortable bringing in our own man to coach.'

"What can you do? You can't run to the fans and say, 'Let's vote on it.' You just have to remember that it can all unravel in a hurry."

Grant was asked if that philosophy translated into fear.

He sees it more as a form of competition.

"You compete against the risks of the job," he said. "It's similar to the competition of playing in a sense, but more than that . . . coaches are much more competitive than players. You either thrive on that competition, or learn to live with it . . . ideally, you do both. But you have to deal with it."

The 1983 season was Grant's seventeenth as coach of the Minnesota Vikings, and his twenty-seventh as a professional head coach. The 1983 season had been less than grand.

Three games into that season, quarterback Kramer was lost to injury. There was sufficient topspin, even without Kramer, to reach midseason with a 6–2 record, but there the topspin ended. The Vikings staggered down the stretch 2–6, having to score a mild upset over Cincinnati in the final game to finish 8–8.

Five weeks after the season ended, on January 28, 1984 . . . and far from Minnesota's ice and snow . . . Grant's retirement was announced in Honolulu, Hawaii.

The announcement was made by Max Winter, the Vikings' president and principal owner. Max lives in Hawaii in the winter, and Max understands Bud.

Besides being tiny and trim and a dapper dresser, Max Winter is a very tough cookie. Like Grant, he is a "business as usual" type, and both men give high marks to resourcefulness and durability. Max is a guy who took his first step toward amassing a considerable fortune by selling used cars in International Falls, Minnesota, which is not at the crossroads of commerce. That was back in the twenties and not all that long before the youthful Grant, growing up in Superior, Wisconsin, which is several lakes south of the Falls, was earning pocket money by crawling into abandoned houses to scavenge lead-pipe for resale.

Pro football's all-star game is the Pro Bowl, and it was played in Honolulu the day following announcement of Bud's retirement. Faced with a breaking news story atop the usual meringue of a Pro Bowl, the network television people interviewed Bud during the game broadcast, which is to say they paid uneasy homage to him.

Network people have never enjoyed a real comfortable fit with Grant. They don't see that much of him for one thing, and for another, they probably don't understand him. Seeing Bud interviewed by a network personality permits images of Jim Bridger, or some other mountain man, being presented at a gathering of socialites. There's respect, to be sure, but what in the world do you do with him, once you have him there?

Anyway, Grant quit.

His decision stunned Minnesotans, delighted opponents, and startled pro football followers everywhere.

How could he just quit?

To be sure, the Viking soup of recent years had been a good deal thinner, but not all of that dilution was of Grant's doing. Grant won. Grant beat you when he should, with almost numbing regularity, and often when he shouldn't. He stood on the sideline, worked that gum, and dealt in realities, always ignoring the emotion that is there, waiting to suck up any coach who will have it.

How could he just walk away?

He had become a part of the game's fabric, essential, and that level lake-ice stare was as identifiable as Shula's firm jaw-set or Landry's snap-brim hat, always perfect for the occasion.

He walked away privately. His decision was made with that same antiseptic sort of logic he has given to his doings since the early days when, for example, he chose to sell only the Sunday newspaper, and then further delineated his market by selling only to those ladies who worked in the bawdy houses along Third Street in his native Superior.

"It was the quickest way I knew of to sell my papers," the logic went. "There were a lot of those ladies . . . remember, Superior was a seaman's town . . . and they all lived in a pretty small area."

As was his practice, Grant took inventory after the 1983 season.

He calls it "doing the sums."

It amounts to a tracking of where the season had, in fact, gone, in relationship to where, in theory, it had been aimed, back in the sultry promise of August. It was a comprehensive inventory.

"It's a review," said Grant, "an opportunity to look at us as coaches, to look at the players, and to see how all of us fit within the system. It's a time to determine where we are meeting goals and where we are falling short. It's also one of the few times when you take your contract out of the drawer and look at it and say, 'How did I come out?' But that's just part of it."

Grant's "sums" sheet had a plus column and a minus column. In recent years, he had taken to adding a third column . . . retirement.

"There has to be more to life than this," he said of coaching. "How long did Bear Bryant coach? I don't know, but it seemed like forever. I'm not sure, though, what all of those years and all of the records availed him. I enjoy coaching . . . it's all I ever wanted to do . . . but I couldn't just sit around and read old newspaper clippings about myself and get a thrill from it."

The retirement column of the sums sheet startled him after the 1983 season.

"Until then, there had always been kids in college, or something else, some demand within our lives that said, 'Not yet.' "

But after the 1983 season, five of the six Grant children were out of school and on their own, and a trust had been established to ensure that Danny, the youngest, would go on to college.

"I hadn't thought of it before," he said, "but we had some protection. It wasn't everything we wanted, but we had protection. Realizing it shocked me . . . maybe I'd just been too busy to look at it, but a lot of my commitment was taken care of."

Being the logical sort, Grant then asked himself a logical question: "Okay, if you retire, what are you going to do?"

As the kids say, no problem.

Bud Grant does not merely enjoy the natural world around us, he cherishes it. He is a hunter and fisherman, but that is as misleading as saying that Indy cars go fast. He loves the outdoors.

Years back, in a conversation given over to sharing enjoyable experiences, Grant talked about sitting in a secluded forest clearing.

"I didn't move, for maybe thirty minutes. At first the only sound was the wind in the trees. After a while, the birds began to call. After that, the squirrels grew comfortable with me and began to move about. I even saw a deer. You have to be patient with nature, that's all."

A football knee had diluted his impact on the racquetball court, but at fifty-six, Grant could still tramp a cornfield for pheasant or cover the marshy ground and tangled brush that always seem to separate the best trout streams from the hard roads.

Finally, there were his terms.

Grant could walk away a winner.

He's a very proud man.

In the many conversations that prefaced these pages, he displayed no more animation than he did when he spoke of a curious thread that has run through his life. . . .

He's always walked away a winner.

"I've been very fortunate, but I don't remember ever leaving something on a losing effort.

"The last time I ever picked up a baseball bat, I hit a home run to win the game in the last inning. We won the last football game I ever played in, and we won the last basketball game I played in. We won the last game of the 1983 season, and that was the only time in all the years with the Vikings we had won the final game of the year."

That was important, leaving on his terms . . . his life has been lived on his terms. He has a very uncluttered view of things, where fact is forever outweighing convention and propriety.

"I had been fortunate. I had worked for twenty-seven years in the only job I ever wanted to have, and I had lived where I wanted to live. How many people get to do that? I couldn't think of another thing I might reasonably expect to gain from staying in coaching."

He worried, briefly, that people might mistake his motives. "To say I'd gotten everything out of coaching that I could might sound selfish to some people," he said. "But I didn't mean it that way." It was a fact, however, and Grant is comfortable with facts . . . he put the worry aside.

He reviewed the possibility of retirement . . . not with other people but with himself. "I sought my own advice," he said.

Advice in hand, he shared it with one person, his wife, Pat.

"She knew I wasn't saying, 'Gosh, help me with this,' " said Grant. "She knew I had thought it through. But Pat was accustomed to being the wife of a coach, and that's not easy. She needed time to think about it, too. I'm sure I don't appreciate the significance of it, but Pat had understood being the coach's wife. She knew the schedule that dominated our life, she understood that the job would take me away from home a lot. She always handled that well . . . Pat excelled in the role my career brought to her."

Pat Grant is fun. She is an affectionate, outgoing, peppy, spontaneous lady who still has a lot of schoolgirl in her. She plays a refreshing counterpoint to Bud's steel-belted individualism.

"People identify the song 'My Way' with Frank Sinatra," said Pat. "I don't . . . it's Bud's song."

Her initial reaction to the issue of retirement was to ask if Bud felt well.

"I feel great," he responded, "that's the point. Why wait until I don't? Or until people say, 'Why doesn't he step aside?' "

The Grants discussed retirement for several days, cautiously at first and then with enthusiasm. "The more we talked," said Bud, "the better it sounded."

Pat Grant's bottom line?

"If you can handle it, I can."

Bud met the next morning with Mike Lynn, general manager of the Vikings.

"I told Mike I wanted to step down as coach," he said.

Bud Grant and Mike Lynn are not similar . . . indeed, one would remind you of the other about like Flin Flon, Manitoba, is remindful of West Palm Beach, Florida.

Bud is direct, a quality that served him well as a coach. Being direct saves time.

Mike is oblique, and that's not a rap. Oblique, means on an angle

. . . not direct. The quality has served Mike well as a general manager, where being direct can get very expensive.

Mike is a negotiator, a bargainer. Negotiators deal in nuances and subtle shadings, and few things in the negotiator's arena are ever quite as they appear to be. Negotiators believe in . . . indeed, they insist on . . . reasons that are supported by "real" reasons.

Mike asked Bud why he wanted to quit.

Grant responded with his sums.

"I told him I had done what I wanted to do, lived where I wanted to live, and enjoyed the experience. I told him I wanted to get out while I was still in good health. Because of my job, there were many things I had wanted to do but had never had time for. I had been forced to live those experiences vicariously. I told him I wanted the opportunity to really experience them."

Mike listened to the "sums" and then asked what it would take to make Grant change his mind.

"I told him that wasn't why I was there . . . I wasn't interested in what it would take," said Bud.

Lynn asked Grant to sleep on his decision and suggested that they meet again the next day.

That's a problem the obliques have with the directs . . . to suggest that Grant sleep on a decision carefully made wasn't really a suggestion at all.

They met the following day, and nothing had changed. Lynn said they should advise Winter and better that they do so in person . . . they agreed to fly to Honolulu on Friday, January 27.

In Honolulu, they went immediately to Max's home near Diamond Head.

"Max was out for a walk," Bud recalled. "We sat out front and waited for him. As he came up the drive, he saw us and said, 'What a surprise.' "

Lynn told Winter that Bud had something to tell him.

"I don't remember the exact words," said Grant, "but it was essentially the same thing I had told Mike. Max may have been surprised initially, but not for long . . . Max recovers quickly."

Was Grant relieved to have the telling behind him?

"I don't think so . . . coaching was never a burden for me, so I didn't leave it with a feeling of relief."

Grant asked that his assistant coaches be retained for another year . . . Winter agreed, and then surprised Bud by asking him to serve out the final year of his contract as a consultant, at least through the period of transition.

"I had planned on flying home and cleaning out my desk," said Grant. "When Max said he wanted to honor the last year of my contract, I thought it was a very nice gesture."

Lynn and Winter then addressed the issue of a replacement . . . their decision was as surprising as it was swift. The job would be offered to Les Steckel, a thirty-eight-year-old assistant on Grant's staff.

Steckel fit the "bright young man at a gallop" profile.

A decorated Marine combat leader in Vietnam, he had coached seven years as a college assistant at Colorado and the Naval Academy. He was on the San Francisco 49er staff for a year, under Pete McCulley, before joining the Viking staff in 1979.

At Minnesota, Steckel had been considered as a candidate for the Dallas Cowboys coaching staff. And he had been offered the University of Minnesota job, but declined.

Steckel was flown out to Hawaii on Saturday, one day after Winter learned of Grant's decision to retire. No one else was interviewed for the job, apparently no one else was considered. Steckel had the job before the day was out and was interviewed as the new coach of the Vikings during the same Pro Bowl broadcast that followed up on Bud's departure.

Grant approved the choice, but the choice was not his.

If Grant has one regret concerning his resignation, it is the way it was introduced to and impacted upon his assistants. Bud had to call them from Hawaii to advise them of his departure and Steckel's promotion.

"The timing and the way it was done were not good," said Grant. "Unfortunately, there wasn't any other way it could have been done."

Jerry Burns, the offensive coordinator, was hardest hit. A Grant assistant since 1968, Burns had interviewed for several NFL jobs and seemed a logical head coaching choice. Distressed by the naming of Steckel, Burns offered to leave, only to be told his input to the new staff would be vital. It wasn't . . . Steckel turned away from Burns's advice shortly after the 1984 season began, thereby depriving himself of one of the league's brightest offensive thinkers.

John Michels, a Grant assistant for twenty-five years at Winnipeg and Minnesota, had turned down a coaching opportunity in Canada the year before. An excellent offensive line coach, Michels was shunted by Steckel to coaching running backs.

Bus Mertes and Bob Hollway, longtime assistants, were spun off by Steckel to research and quality control, which translates in some circles to grading films and looking out the window.

Les Steckel was the youngest head coach in the National Football League and a man possessed of a bristling motivational zeal. He would arm his players with that same zeal. He was a surprise choice, unknown for the most part on the broad canvas of the industry. And he relished the opportunity.

But he didn't take.

For an avalanche of reasons, some of his own design and others visited upon him by the fates, his team collapsed. Under Grant for seventeen seasons, the Vikings had won and lost but they had never been an embarrassment. Under Steckel, they became one. Disenchanted at the course of things, Burns announced near midyear that he intended to resign. The bottom fell out after that. At a home game in late November, with the traditionally beatable Chicago Bears flogging the Vikings 34–3, a banner was stretched in one end zone of the Metrodome.

It read, "Grant us one wish . . . come back, Bud!"

Grant didn't see that banner . . . he was at the family lake home in Wisconsin, deer hunting with one of his sons. He hunted and fished and was available in his role of executive consultant for organizational development.

"What do you do?" he was asked.

"I listen," he said. "If someone needs to talk something out . . . take an idea out of their head and see how another person will respond to it . . . well, I'm a good listener.

"Ultimately, people have to make their own decisions, but sometimes it helps if you can play them off someone you're comfortable with, someone you know isn't going to try to influence you or carry things outside the office. That's what I do, I'm a sounding board."

And a very discreet one.

"I made a point of staying away from the team," he said. "I didn't go to training camp, and I didn't watch practice. I like to have free space, and I figured they should have it, too. And, besides, I didn't ever want to put myself in a position where people could ask, 'You're around them all the time, what's really going on?' "

As the Viking season unraveled, Grant was asked by an acquaintance if he would consider returning.

"No." End of discussion.

As Grant was dropping off that same acquaintance at the Minneapolis–St. Paul airport, a man leaving the terminal recognized him.

"Hey, Bud!" he shouted . . . loud enough that several people turned to stare.

"We miss you, Bud . . . man, do we miss you!"

The Vikings would end the 1984 season on Sunday, December 16, at home against Green Bay. They were 3–12 going into that final game.

On Wednesday preceding the finale, Lynn asked Grant to meet with him.

Mike asked if Bud would return as coach.

"Absolutely not," said Grant, "you have a coach."

Borrowing a line from an earlier meeting, Mike asked what it would take to make Grant reconsider.

"I told him I wasn't interested. I pointed out they'd had a lot of injuries, and they'd had to make do without their quarterback. [Kramer had been hurt for a second year in succession.] I told him we hadn't been through anything like this before . . . we'd been spoiled, really. A lot of teams go through that sort of fire far more regularly than the Vikings had. It isn't easy, but sometimes you have to ride out the hard times, too. I told him I didn't think Les had been given an opportunity to prove what he could do."

Lynn raised the question again on Thursday.

And Friday.

Grant wouldn't hear of it.

On Saturday, the day before the final game, Lynn told Grant the club's directors had met and had decided to let Steckel go, regardless of the outcome of the game with Green Bay.

"I told him I was sorry to hear that," said Grant. "It had been a difficult year . . . for the first time, people were making jokes about the Vikings. In their frustration, people can be cruel. That had not happened to the Vikings before . . . we'd always had great support, regardless of how we were doing."

Lynn said the directors wanted Bud to return as coach.

"I told him there was nothing I wanted that I would return to coaching for," said Grant. The weekend was an unpleasant one for Grant.

"Because it was Green Bay, and I'm from Wisconsin and still spend a lot of time there, I had to deal with all the normal things, people calling for tickets and wanting to visit. And, all the while, I knew what was going to happen."

What happened Sunday was another loss . . . the Vikings finished 3–13, more losses than any club in franchise history.

On Monday morning, Steckel went to the office to meet with his staff, unaware the decision on him had already been made. Lynn called him in and asked for his resignation . . . when Steckel refused to resign, he was fired. That afternoon, following a press conference to announce Steckel's departure, Lynn again sought out Grant.

This time, with an offer.

"I could coach for as long as I wanted," said Grant. "Mike called it a lifetime contract."

If the contract's tenure was unique, its benefits weren't far behind.

"I've never been one to look very far down the road," said Grant. "What Mike proposed took care of down the road. It would take care of us, it would take care of Pat if something happened to me."

If this makes any sense, the money was good, but the fact that it removed concern for the future was even better.

"There are other coaches who make more money than I do," said

Grant. "That's fine . . . I've always felt that living where you want to live is worth more than dollars. Everything I value in life is here. If you said, go to New York or Los Angeles and name your price, I wouldn't be interested."

Grant doesn't volunteer terms of his contract. When he left coaching after the 1983 season, he was believed to be comfortably within the upper middle of the NFL's salary level for head coaches, estimated at between $200,000 and $300,000 per year. The new contract is believed to have exceeded those figures by far.

From the Viking standpoint, the salary numbers probably were the most easily solved part of the predicament. The season just ended had spawned a momentum new to professional football in Minnesota, a momentum that threatened to carry fans away from the Vikings. There was one obvious way in which to restore the public confidence in the organization . . . bring back Grant.

Bud made notes on Lynn's proposal, took them home, and for the second time in less than a year talked about the future with Pat Grant. He wanted to be sure both of them, if that was to be the choice, returned as they had left, with their eyes wide open.

"I explained the offer to Pat," he said, "but we really talked more in terms of what going back would mean. I told her that if we went back, it would be for a relatively short period of time . . . and with the realization that the team we would take over might not be any better than it had been in 1984."

Remove money from the equation, and there seemed to be precious little reason for returning or even to consider returning.

Kramer, the quarterback and cornerstone of the offense, had missed nearly all of the past two seasons, giving real question to his future. The nucleus of proven players was not large, and many within its membership had become disenchanted during the season without Grant.

The future, Grant realized, was less promising than it had been with the patchwork team he inherited in 1967.

All of that calm and unruffled surface notwithstanding, Bud Grant is a man with an ego.

"You can't be in this business without one," he said. "You couldn't sustain yourself in a job like this without being able to take satisfaction in your accomplishments."

Fine . . . but why go back?

Grant the pragmatist would cringe at the mention of noble thoughts, but by the same token, Grant the pragmatist knew that whatever mark he had carved had been due, in great part, to the opportunity afforded him by the Vikings.

A debt?

No way . . . he had given to the Vikings in equal measure.

Loyalty, then?

Not in the strict sense.

Try "resentment" . . . or even "anger."

Grant, more than anyone else, had been responsible for lifting the Vikings, first to respectability and then on to prominence. Ask anyone in this business to name the four or five coaches most held in respect. Grant will be one of them.

What had happened to the Vikings in 1984 troubled him deeply. Not the record so much. Having been a coach for such a long time, he knew that the number of wins and losses didn't necessarily give an accurate reflection of effort made. What nettled Bud was the fact that the team . . . indeed, the Viking name . . . was being held up to public ridicule.

In retrospect, Grant's decision to return seemed based upon his being able to fit the pieces together, and upon the fact that the fit was made on his terms.

He would coach for as long as he wanted to.

He would work for benefits he never would have dreamed of . . . not bad, for a fellow who, by his own admission, might well have ended up working ore boats out of Superior.

Finally, he would coach for the good name of this team that he had built.

After that 1984 season of disarray, Bud talked about how the team was the butt of every saloon joke in town. His tone in the telling made his anger apparent. He also examined the risk of his being exposed to that sort of thing by returning to coaching.

"Being called a horse's ass wouldn't devastate me," he said. "All I can do is the very best I can . . . I can live with that, however it works out."

The Grants explored their options.

"We knew we weren't going in with a five-year plan, setting long-term goals," said Bud. "We knew we wouldn't be taking a team from here to there, on the long haul. I was under no illusions . . . they wanted me to come back to keep the ship afloat . . . to use my 'whatever' as much as my coaching abilities."

The "whatever" Grant referred to may be replaced with words like "credibility" or "charisma" . . . agency types call it sizzle.

"I think we recognized the pitfalls," said Bud. "It still seemed worthwhile."

Pat Grant was, according to her husband, surprised when he left coaching but less surprised when he returned.

"She never really got into the swing of my not coaching," he said. "You have to understand, Pat's a real diehard fan. She's been watching games and cheering for so many years . . . games I played in or coached, all of the kids' games. She enjoys football. I don't really think she understands it, but she enjoys it. We sat together at the Viking games when I was out of coaching . . . she talks too much during a game, but she really does enjoy it. The criticism the team took that year bothered her a lot."

"Do you want to go back?" Pat Grant asked her husband.

Bud said he thought he did.

"Fine," said Pat, "let's go."

Grant called Mike Lynn at home and made an acceptance that was as unusual as it was brief.

"I told him I'd come back, and then I told him to start looking for my replacement. I said that, if they had someone in mind and wanted him on the staff, to let me know. But I said they should start looking and start looking now."

The next night, an overflow press conference awaited the announcement of the new Viking coach.

Grant was late . . . his youngest son, Danny, had a high school basketball game that night, and the game went to overtime. Danny's team won, but Bud wouldn't leave before the game ended.

Priorities.

His mother, Bernice Grant, lives in California now with one of Bud's brothers. She was asked what Bud was like when he was a little boy.

Her tone was ladylike, but still made it obvious that was a silly question.

"Why, the same as he is today," she answered. "He hasn't changed . . . Bud has been his own person since the day he was born."

Over and back . . . Grant had coached the Vikings, left the Vikings, and then returned to coach again. The 1985 NFL season, Grant's twenty-eighth as a head coach, began so grandly with the win over the 49ers. Then it bobbed and weaved through the jarring challenges of October and November. It featured last-second failures, but it also featured heroic efforts. Too frequently, what happened on the field was played against a dreary counterpoint of front-office spite. Less was written and said of how the Vikings did on the field than of what went on in the board room.

And then the 1985 season ended . . . and that was interesting, too.

2

Superior

They are called Twin Ports, but Duluth, Minnesota, and Superior, Wisconsin, are as poorly matched as a good china teacup and a battered old tin saucer.

The two cities lie at the heel of Lake Superior, linked by the high bridge and separated by more than water.

"Growing up in Superior," said Bud Grant, "gave you a complex. We were down on the water, and if we looked to Duluth, we had to look up. Duluth was on the hill."

Duluth, then, was the more attractive city?

"Definitely."

And Superior?

"Superior . . ." Grant paused, weighing his response. "Superior was a tough place to live."

Not that Duluth was a spa of easy living. The point is a relative one. The Twin Ports, looked-up-to Duluth included, were shipping towns.

Time was, they sent the iron ore and the prairie grain around the Great Lakes horn and on to the world. The Mesabi iron range, rich and red and thought to run forever, lay north and west of Duluth on the Minnesota end of the lake.

Turned out, though, that the Mesabi didn't run forever. The range Minnesotans had proudly called inexhaustible died of exhaustion, and now the ore boats round a far greater horn, coming from the other side of the world. Prairie wheat remained the gut of Twin Ports shipping, but its iron heart faltered, its passing wedged between world wars and a great depression. Both towns suffered, but Superior the more . . . it was truly the working man's town, grimy and out at the elbows, its shoulder forever hunched against the chill wind whipping off the lake.

17

"We all remember bits and pieces of our childhood," said Grant. "When I remember Superior, there is the lakefront, the cold, the dirt, and the wind . . . always, the wind."

Harry Peter Grant, Jr., was born there on May 20, 1927.

Times being what they were, Harry Peter Grant, Sr., received his fireman's wages in scrip, as opposed to conventional greenbacks. The trouble with scrip was that no more than half the town's merchants would honor it.

This is not to suggest, however, that annoyances like worthless currency ever set Harry Grant back very far.

"Gregarious." That was Bud's answer when asked to describe his father.

Odd, the son who would become known across the land by descriptives such as "cold" and "remote" and even "glacial" had a bonafide extrovert for a father.

"He was the sort who would have bought the first round of beers at the tavern," said Bud. "He was a hearty, outgoing fellow who truly enjoyed being with his friends. He was very much a man's man.

"I didn't know what the word meant then, but my father had a great rapport with people. Everybody in Superior knew Harry Grant. If we walked down the street, he had a greeting for everybody we passed, and he had a remarkable gift, I think, in that he always found something cheerful to say. He wasn't a knocker. If you weren't a positive thinker, you wouldn't have had much in common with my dad."

Grant flashed the grin that can have such shock value, because it is so at odds with the sober expression he usually shows.

"I took after my mother," he said.

He was the first born of Harry and Bernice Grant. The Grants lived on First Street, hard by the waterfront. Bud's mother had grown up in Duluth. His father was the son of a lumberjack, born near Odanah, east of Superior.

A daughter followed Bud, but died at birth. Two more sons, Jim and Jack, were born to the Grants, but Bud was the oldest by seven years, a gap too great for much sharing.

"I baby-sat my brothers a lot, but we were never really close," Grant said.

And on becoming "Bud?"

"My mother didn't care for the confusion of having two Harrys under the same roof. She took to calling me Buddy Boy. As I grew, the name got shorter."

He was asked to name a strong memory of his youth.

"Being hungry. I remember never having as much to eat as I would have liked. I don't mean we went hungry . . . there was food on the table . . . I'm talking about being able to eat the way a kid likes to eat, which means all you want. If three of us were eating, there were three pork chops, never four or five.

"I loved Thanksgiving and Christmas because I knew there would be leftovers."

Grant frowned and chided himself.

"Talking, I'm making it sound terrible. It wasn't . . . I had a great childhood. Those were the times, really, the depression. We weren't well-off, but no one we knew was well-off. And I had fun."

How?

"Imagination, mostly . . . that and a set of Lincoln Logs."

He paused for a moment. "Kids, today, have so many 'tools' to keep them entertained. The problem with that is, when we shower them with things, we cover up their imagination.

"We had this big old radio . . . I think it was an Arvin. It worked about half the time, but I don't think anybody we knew had a radio that worked all the time. I listened to that radio a lot . . . radio was aided greatly by imagination."

If Bud's father was gregarious, he also was imaginative.

"My dad worked twenty-four hours on and twenty-four hours off at the fire hall, and he always had some sort of a scheme for making extra money. He had a bingo stand he'd take around to the church fairs and picnics . . . I can remember going to sleep on the ground under the bingo stand. Then he had the concession stand at the Superior Blues baseball park. If there were hotdogs left over after a game, my job was to take them out of the kettle, dry them off, and put them away for the next game. We had a lot of noodles when I was young, and I'm not very fond of noodles to this day. I don't eat hot-dogs, either."

Grant contracted polio when he was young.

That admission was vintage Bud Grant.

Q: How did you get started in sports?

A: Got a push from a doctor, actually.

Q: How was that?

A: I had polio when I was a kid. I don't think people knew a lot about polio then . . . at least they didn't know much about it in Superior. I don't think they knew I had it until after the fact.

Q: What did it do to you?

A: Left me with one leg shorter than the other.

Q: Then what happened?

A: Our doctor was an old fellow named Simcock . . . I believe he was ahead of his time. My parents went to him, and I think they were expecting special procedures for my rehabilitation . . . massages or baths or things like that. I think they wanted to pamper me.

Q: So what happened?

A: Doc Simcock said the best therapy they could give me was a ball and a glove . . . he told them to let me be active, like any other kid.

Harry Grant, Sr., had been one of Superior's best town players. "I have scrapbooks," said Bud. "He played for three or four teams, and he always hit .400 or better." Bud's father didn't have the price of a new baseball glove, so he gave him his old one, and a young athlete was launched, although not without typical candor.

"I started in baseball," he said, "but you have to understand about Superior. You're never really sure winter's over until June, so it makes for a very short baseball season. I spent most of my time playing football and basketball."

By the time he was in the seventh grade, Bud was organizing schoolboy football games between neighborhoods. "We didn't have school teams at that age, so I was the one who called kids from another school and made arrangements. I even made out our lineup."

Another interest was growing in young Grant at the time, and it would prove to be an abiding one . . . his interest in the outdoors.

"I think you must be born with a love of nature," he said. "I believe I was. My father was not . . . he'd go out some, but hunting or fishing or just being out there weren't really important to him.

"I can see the same thing in my family . . . the boys don't necessarily have the same feelings I do."

The lack of that feeling among his friends meant that young Grant often spent days alone.

"Saturdays and Sundays, I would break down my .22, stow it in my newspaper sack, and ride the bus out to the end of the line. I'd hunt rabbits all day long. Every once in a while, I'd have a friend along, but more often I was by myself. My buddies were more interested in girls and in working on old cars."

Did Grant ever bend in those social directions favored by his friends?

"I tried, but the results weren't too spectacular. I took the dancing lessons at the Y, along with everybody else. Keep in mind, though, that I was six feet three when I was a freshman in high school, my full height. I also couldn't dance a lick then and can't now. If the girls of our class have a strong memory of me, it's probably for stepping on their feet."

Did he have a girlfriend in high school?

"Nope. I walked girls home from the drugstore a time or two, but I didn't date."

What did Bud do while his classmates went to dances and parties?

"Spent a lot of time at the pool hall, as I remember."

Why?

"I was shy."

That shyness, however, did not carry over onto the athletic field . . . although the first order of business was to put a muzzle on his "advance man."

"My father liked to brag on me," said Bud. "He more or less previewed my arrival in high school football . . . he called me kid, and he was fond of talking to our high school coach and saying, 'Wait'll you see my kid.' "

Up to a point, Harry Grant did that.

"He came to my first football practice at Central High School," Bud recalled.

"I was out on the field, doing something, and the next thing I knew, there he was, talking to the coach. I knew what he was saying."

In the telling, Grant's tone took on the chill a thousand football players would come to recognize in later years. Not angry, not threatening . . . just very clear and deliberate, so that there would be absolutely no margin for misunderstanding his meaning.

"I went home that night," he said, "and I told my dad, 'Don't you ever come to practice again.' "

Did he?

"No."

(Pat Grant giggled when she heard this. "Well, then, I'll bet he peeked through the fence," she said.)

Bud admired his father, but they were not similar.

"We were close, but not in the usual father-son relationship . . . it was more man-to-man. He was always very supportive of me, but he didn't try to offer direction or steer my course for me. He just supported me."

And impacted upon Bud's life.

"When he died, I received letters from a lot of people who knew my dad," Bud said. "I remember one. It was written by a fellow who was in prison. He said that my dad had been an influence in his life, and he was grateful to him. He said he would be getting out soon, but if it hadn't been for my dad, he would have been dead by then."

Bud got into the football games as a high school freshman, but always as a reserve. He played fullback.

"I got into every game except the last one," he said. "We played LaCrosse, and I sat on the bench the whole night. I was crushed."

While banished from the practice field, Harry Grant still had access to the games. He asked Coach Harry Conley why Bud hadn't played.

"He told my dad he was saving me for the basketball season," said Bud. "I thought that was the most ridiculous reason I'd ever heard of."

In retrospect, Coach Conley's reasoning wasn't all bad. By the fourth game of the basketball season, freshman Grant was a starter.

"I'm not sure that was a distinction," said Bud. "I think we only won five or six games during the regular season."

But then a modest bolt of Upper Midwest lightning touched the Central High cagers toward the end of Grant's freshman year . . . they started to win.

"Late in the season, I remember one of the players saying that if we kept going good, we might win some games in the tournament. I didn't even know there was a tournament."

There was . . . at the University of Wisconsin field house in Madison. And the cinderella Vikings from Central High were in it.

"I'd never been that far away from Superior," said Bud. "We ate in a cafeteria on campus . . . I can still remember how I felt, the first time I saw all that food. I think I ate five or six meals a day."

And Central won games it had little business winning, losing out, in the semifinals, in overtime.

The team returned to Superior and to a celebration. Shortly after that, Bud fell ill, running a high fever. "That was when my hair started to turn gray," Grant said. He was not yet fifteen years old.

Bud advanced through schoolboy athletics with distinction, although still with the limp brought on by polio. He lost the limp after high school. He won conference and regional honors for his play in football and basketball. His American Legion baseball career was noteworthy also; between his junior and senior years he was named to *Esquire* magazine's East–West high school all-star game and played in Comiskey Park, Chicago. Bud rode the train to Chicago.

"I did the usual dumb things a country kid does when he goes to the big city," Grant recalled. Among them, the ignorance of the fact that one puts the shower curtain inside the tub when one takes a shower. "I flooded out the hotel room on the floor beneath me," he said.

The all-stars had five pitchers to a team, and they had pitch-offs to see who would start. Grant started for his team. "But I'd thrown so much, getting the start, that I didn't have much left. But I hit two balls into the seats in batting practice."

How do quiet, shy people come to excel as athletes?

"You can compete without causing a racket," said Grant. "I never have thought much of players who have to be loud and show a tough-guy image.

"I am a competitive person. I've never enjoyed losing, not at anything. If I had some success, it probably was because I never doubted myself. I believed I could play longer and work harder than anybody I might go up against. I never got tired. I could run every play of a football game, and I could run up and down a basketball court all night. I didn't get tired.

"I think I understood that, and knew what it meant," said Grant. "I didn't hope I could do it, I knew I could. If I played against you, I knew I could wear you down . . . it might take a long time, but I knew that eventually I was going to win."

Did he train as an athlete?

"I don't remember ever trying to get into shape, and I don't remember being out of shape. I ran everywhere I went. We lived a mile from school, I ran there and back. If I was out at night and a couple of miles from home, I'd give myself ten minutes to run it. I'm not a jogger, I've got poor knees, but I think I understand when they talk of a feeling of freedom that comes with running past a certain point. I loved to run."

He also worked.

"Summers, we were on the docks, trimming grain. You worked in the hold of a ship, wearing a mask against the dust, while grain was pumped into the hold. Walk grain in the hold of a ship and keep it level with a scoop, and you won't have to worry about being in shape."

Much of Bud's running was done with a football under his arm.

By the conclusion of his senior football season, he had drawn the attention of college scouts from Iowa, Minnesota, Northwestern, and Wisconsin. Conley, his high school coach, didn't let the attention get the best of young Grant.

"When an athlete gets recognition, and I did, it isn't just the athlete who has to cope with it . . . his coach has to be able to handle it, too. Coach Conley did that. He was very tough but very fair, too. He kept my feet on the ground."

There is a bittersweet refrain to Grant's memories of Superior.

"It's one of those towns people are from," he said. "As soon as they could, people moved on."

Including his parents.

After Bud had gone on to Canada, the Grants went to California to attend the funeral of a relative. "After they got back, all they could talk about was how there were flowers blooming out there in February . . . in Superior, there was two feet of snow on the car, and it didn't start all that often.

"Moving to California became their goal. My dad took early retirement, they sold the house, and headed west.

"My dad was dead within two years."

There is enough of Grant in his reaction to that tragedy to pay attention.

"I think they would have been better off staying in Superior. My dad would have had to battle the winter, but at least he would have had something to battle. And in Superior, he knew people . . . he was somebody. In California, he was just another retiree from the Midwest. Going there deprived him of purpose."

Bud once told an acquaintance that, had it not been for athletics, he might well have ended up working as a hand on the freighters out of Superior port.

"That's a roundabout way of saying I didn't apply myself to schoolwork the way I should have," he said. "I questioned a lot of it. If I didn't see the sense in a course, I didn't take it seriously. If a course made sense, I worked at it . . . in geometry, as I recall, I got perfect marks."

Textbooks weren't the only thing keeping Grant from looking very far down the road.

"I spent my high school years preparing, in my mind, to go to war," he said. "If you were coming out of school then [1945], the war was a very real part of your future. Fellows I went to school with and played ball with went off to war. There were some who didn't come back."

Did the prospect frighten him?

"I don't think so. I was interested in it . . . I used to follow the dispatches in the newspaper. The paper would have little maps every day, with arrows showing how far the allied troops had advanced or pointing out the site of a particular battle. When I went to the movies, I was as interested in the newsreel as I was in the feature."

The prospect of going to war wasn't alien to Grant . . . in a way, he saw it as another level of competition. He felt he was prepared, mentally and physically. "I wanted to be something special," said Bud. "I told myself I would be the best soldier or the best sailor or the best aviator.

"Young people, today, wouldn't understand this, but I was disappointed when the war ended. I wasn't sorry to see the killing and suffering halted, but I was saddened that I would miss the experience of being a part of it."

Did the young Grant ever dream of fortune?

"We had a mail-order catalog," he said. "I can still see this one page . . . it had an expensive hunting knife and hatchet. I used to dream about how it would feel to walk into the catalog store and order both of them at the same time.

"I'd say to myself, 'Now, if I could ever do that. . . .' "

3

Great Lakes

It almost has the look of a college campus, with its winding, tree-lined avenues. Lawns are fiercely tended, and the buildings are old and handsome, many built of deep-red brick.

The Great Lakes Naval Training Center was a school for sailors, and in the 1940s, its students majored in war.

Still do, of course, although on a scale not nearly so grand . . . the war business has changed over the years, the emphasis having swung from mighty armadas to a sleek, swift nuclear navy.

It's still there, operative, on the wind-raked shore of Lake Michigan . . . north of the Chicago Loop by some fifty miles.

But it's changed.

The wooden bleachers that marked Ross Field are long torn down. There's no more football at Great Lakes, not the serious kind, anyway . . . the Ross area is a parade ground now, with a reviewing stand where one of the end zones used to be and a stand of maples at the other, of a size to remind you how many years have gone by since the Bluejackets savaged Notre Dame in a memorable final game.

If you are interested enough to climb the tight, winding staircase to the top floor of the administration building, you can still leaf through bound volumes of the *Bluejacket,* the base newspaper, pages crackling and discolored.

A copy from July 1945 carried a small item near the bottom of the page, boxed like a classified ad: "Candidates for the football team meet Lt. (JG) P. Brown in the Gear Locker, Building 211. Candidates are to have plays on the board copied in notebooks by the time the coach arrives."

Bud Grant was at Great Lakes for the better part of a year . . . he arrived ready to accept his role in the war, and departed in confusion and haste, an unwitting embarrassment to a service that acted by overreacting.

25

Bud graduated from high school and left Superior for Great Lakes on July 6, 1945. Bill Blank, his closest chum through high school, went into the service when Bud did, but Blank went into the army.

Bud's mother asked him why he had selected the navy.

"You know your bed's going to be in the same place every night," he explained.

One month later, on August 6, 1945, the first atomic bomb to be used in warfare fell on Hiroshima, Japan. The end of the war was at hand, even as Bud entered boot camp.

But his arrival had not gone unnoticed.

Harry Stuhldreher, the football coach at Wisconsin, was trying to recruit Grant. When he learned that Bud had joined the navy, Stuhldreher wrote to a friend, the coach of the Great Lakes Naval Training Center football team.

Paul Brown.

This business, professional football, has been given form and substance by a mixed bag of artisans, which probably makes it quite a bit like the business you're in. There have been pluggers and plodders, uninspired types and "get rich quick" hustlers. The bad guys and the good guys, the selfless and the selfish.

But every now and then, someone special comes along . . . just as, every now and then, a Hemingway decides to put words on paper or a Berlin decides to put words to music.

Those people are the master builders of their industries, and Paul Brown was one of them.

As a high school coach, as a college coach, as a professional coach . . . Brown set standards of excellence for others to measure themselves against.

Unruffled, aloof, precise, demanding, brilliant.

His football was a painstaking exercise in tactics and strategy . . . a meticulous choreography that just happened to involve huge men in gaudy costumes, hurtling themselves against one another.

Go to anyone in our business and say, "P.B."

They'll know who you're talking about.

In the summer of 1945, Lt. Paul Brown noted the letter from his friend Stuhldreher about "a young kid from the northwoods of Wisconsin" as he prepared to form his football team.

Brown and Grant would become well-acquainted, initially by chance, later out of mutual respect. Chance, in this case, had to do with a misguided dentist.

But only after the rowing.

Three days into boot camp, Grant read a notice on the company bulletin board. Tryouts would be held for the battalion crews competition. Grant didn't know what a crew was, so he asked. He learned that crews row. He signed up. Having grown up on Lake Superior, he was no stranger to rowing a boat. More to the point, men chosen for the crew would be exempt from KP. And if you don't know what KP means, find an old man and ask him.

Crewing at Great Lakes bore no resemblance to that fine old sport as it is practiced at eastern universities. Rather than sleek shells, the sailors at Great Lakes crewed deep, heavy, unwieldly whale boats.

"We sat six to a side," said Bud, "and the boat was so deep you couldn't see over the side when you were in your stroke. And we had fixed seats . . . just regular benches. In a real crewing shell, as I understand it, the seat moves with you in your stroke. In the whale boats, the only thing that moved was your butt, rubbing against the planks. I was sitting on blisters . . . big blisters . . . after a week of rowing."

And after two weeks, Grant's crew competed in the Commander's Cup series.

"It was a big thing," he recalled. "It was a Saturday, a bright, hot day. There was a band playing, people sitting in bleachers, and all of the brass was there watching."

The crews set out, dressed in summer whites. By the halfway point of the race, Grant could see the blood on the trousers of the man sitting in front of him as his blisters broke. "From the feeling, I knew mine had broken, too.

"I have never been so tired in my life," said Bud. "We were on the home leg of the course, and our coxswain picked up the stroke. We couldn't see a thing . . . we just rowed. The coxswain would shout, 'Just one more stroke!' He must have said that a hundred times. I remember thinking that I'd peel potatoes for a month if I could just rest for a minute."

Grant's boat won . . . and had steak dinner in the officer's mess.

The following Monday, Bud received word that he was to report for football practice. He and a handful of other recruits boarded a bus each morning, went "mainside" for football, and returned to boot camp at night.

Actually, Bud was splitting his time between football and the dental clinic.

"I never really did understand it," Grant said, "but they were forming a dental company . . . people who needed a lot of work on their teeth. I can remember getting my teeth worked on in the afternoon and spitting blood into a bucket all night. Then, the dentist who was working on me told me he was going to pull all my teeth."

Grant told one of the assistant football coaches, Blanton Collier (who later coached the Browns). Collier had Bud see another dentist, Les Horvath, who had been an All-American back at Ohio State.

"Horvath said I needed some work, but I didn't need to have any teeth pulled. Then Blanton went to Paul Brown and told him about it."

Brown was furious . . . furious enough, that he went to see the errant dentist.

"Paul was a very well-ordered and logical individual," said Grant. "I think it shocked him that someone would contemplate doing something so drastic without cause. I found out that he said to Blanton, 'What are they doing? He's just a kid!' Knowing Paul, he probably had that dentist shipped overseas."

Within three weeks, Grant was moved out of the boot company and over "mainside," with the football team.

He was one of 300 candidates for a football team that, in those days, ranked as a powerhouse. Many college and professional players were still in military service . . . teams fielded at installations like Great Lakes, Fort Sill, and El Toro were among the strongest in the country.

Grant was one of a half-dozen lads straight out of high school who were serious candidates to play. Another was an apple-cheeked halfback from Anoka, Minnesota, named Billy Bye. Grant knew about Bye before he arrived at Great Lakes . . . they had played against one another in football. Superior, the legendary Wisconsin state champion, played at Anoka, the legendary Minnesota champion, in a special Halloween game. Anoka won.

"We had tackling practice before we did anything else," Bud recalled. "We were supposed to rotate, work against a different guy every time up, but I always seemed to end up paired against this one guy, who was absolutely huge."

A fullback in high school, Grant started toward the fullback line when the coaches told candidates to assemble at their positions.

"There was this guy again, he was standing at the head of the fullback line," said Bud. "When I saw him, I decided I wasn't a fullback anymore . . . I kept on walking and lined up with the ends."

The fullback of Bud's memory was Marion Motley, an amiable bear of a man, who went on, under Brown, to become a great star with the Cleveland Browns.

The team practiced two months before the season ever began.

"We got up in the morning, had chow, went to meeting, practiced, had chow, went to meeting, practiced, had chow, and went to bed," said Grant. "That was our day."

Brown's assistant coaches were Collier and a jaunty little officer named Wilbur Ewbank, who would go on to fame as Weeb Ewbank, coach of the New York Jets and Baltimore Colts . . . the only man to win championships in both the AFL and the NFL.

How did it seem to you, being a kid fresh out of high school, competing with guys who were college All-Americans and stars in the pros?

"I don't know that I gave it much thought," said Grant. "It was football practice, and I was no stranger to football practice. I found out, early on, that I could catch the ball as well as most of the people we had."

Paul Brown's approach to football made an impression on Grant.

"He was as serious about it there, I'm sure, as he was when he coached the Browns to all those victories. And being in the service, in a situation like that, you were bound to have a certain number of people who didn't take it as seriously as he did. It didn't matter whether you were a nobody, or whether you were a big name . . . if you gave it the 'haw' around Paul, you were gone."

Players had their assigned seats in the meeting room. If you went to meeting and there was no name on your chair, that meant you were gone. They had playbooks, and they were responsible for copying the plays Brown drew on the board. Brown checked the books regularly.

"I remember the first trip we took," said Bud. "When we got up in the morning, there was a newspaper outside the door of every room, and waiters brought an extra large orange juice with the wake-up call. We had a travel itinerary . . . I didn't even know what the word meant."

What was Paul Brown like?

"Like he is now . . . stern, at least on the surface. He would laugh, but it was almost an embarrassed laugh . . . it sort of backed away."

And he could be tough.

"We had some old salts on the team, and they decided to test Brown's rules . . . they went out one night and tied one on."

The next day at practice, Grant said, Coach Brown called the culprits out in front of the squad. He told them it was his opinion that they had violated the conduct rules of the football team.

"Get away, get far away from me," the coach said, "and do it now."

"By the time we got back to the barracks that afternoon, their gear was gone, and they were gone," said Grant. "There was nothing, absolutely nothing, to suggest they had ever been a part of us . . . it was as if they had never been there."

Great Lakes scrimmaged with the College All-Star team, led by Michigan All-American Tommy Harmon. The All-Stars were coached by a man Grant would come to know in future years, Minnesota's Bernie Bierman.

Collier, the offensive coach, sent Grant into that scrimmage with a play that was a Paul Brown pet, TD-90.

"I went deep on a post pattern," said Bud. "I made the catch and scored."

At midseason, the Bluejackets were playing Central Michigan, and Brown once again called on TD-90.

The pass went to Grant for an apparent touchdown, but a penalty call against Great Lakes nullified the play. Again Brown called for the pass play, and again Grant made the catch and went on to score. And again a penalty was called.

"He was fuming," Bud said of Brown. "He thought penalties were inexcusable. By that time, I guess, he was determined to make TD-90 work . . . he called it a third straight time. I made another catch for a touchdown, and that one stood up.

"Paul was laughing and shouting, 'Good going!' when I got to the bench. It pleased him that he could force that play to be a success."

Great Lakes played Notre Dame in the final game of the 1945 season, the last to be played on the post. More than 30,000 persons crowded the wooden bleachers of Ross Field. The Fighting Irish, led by Angelo Bertelli, were favored.

Great Lakes won the game, 19–7. A forty-year-old copy of the *Bluejacket* newspaper cited "Able Seaman Harry Grant, one of the heroes of an inspired Great Lakes defense. . . ."

Blanton Collier later relayed a story to Grant of Paul Brown singling him out for praise after the Notre Dame game.

"Blanton said Brown was showing the film to a group of post officers, and he said, 'Boy, did Brown ever rave about you.' I'd gotten knocked down on a play, but got up to make the tackle at a time when we really needed to stop them," said Bud.

What did Grant take away from his football experiences at Great Lakes?

"I learned more about people than anything else from Brown," he said. "He excelled at evaluating people, recognizing what they could and couldn't do. He was able to get the right player into the situation that was right for him. And Paul was both fair and tough . . . you had to prove it to him, and it didn't matter who you were."

Through Brown, Grant began to appreciate the role of the head coach . . . not only the evaluation of players, but utilization of his assistant coaches. "He gave the assistants a lot of leeway, but you never once doubted that Paul was in charge. If I had to sum up briefly, I'd say he was well-organized, he had a gift for saying exactly what he wanted to say, and he said it in very few words."

Sound familiar?

The pro football winds would blow Brown and Grant in different directions, but a bond had been formed.

"When I played for the Eagles and he was coaching the Browns, he'd always come running across the field after the game to shake my hand . . . and for Paul, that was unusual. I think he had a special feeling for the Great Lakes team. I know I did, and I was always grateful to have played for him."

Basketball still followed football, even in the navy . . . Grant turned out for the Bluejacket squad, which was coached by Weeb Ewbank.

Bud laughed.

"Weeb is a wonderful person," he said, "but I think it's a fair statement to say he knew less about basketball than any coach I was ever around. His assistant, Mel Reby, did all the work . . . we'd turn out for practice, and Weeb would wander over to the stands, sit down, and fall asleep."

Bud was a starter for the Great Lakes team before the season was half over. He ended up as the leading rebounder. Great Lakes played DePaul and Loyola and other strong college teams in the area. One young seaman who showed promise before an illness sidelined him was Ara Parseghian.

Following the basketball season, Bud tried out for the post baseball team . . . and became a victim of his own achievement.

"One of the Chicago papers ran a feature article on me as the young sailor who played well in three sports at Great Lakes," he said. "I hadn't really thought about it . . . I was there, and the sports were there, so I competed. I'd been doing that since I started high school. But the story prompted letters of protest from people who said it wasn't fair that I stayed at Great Lakes, playing sports, while their sons were still being sent overseas."

If the readers were angered, so was the object of their wrath. "I never asked anybody for special treatment," said Bud.

"I was called in by this company officer," Bud said. "He told me he was sorry, but I was being transferred, shipped to California. He said there wasn't anything he could do about it."

Grant went to the Treasure Island naval station at San Francisco.

"I was the recreation room orderly," he said. "I racked pool balls and put magazines back in the rack."

For three months.

"I got pretty sour on it," said Bud. "If I had been doing something worthwhile, it would have been different. But I wasn't . . . and I wanted out."

He saw a directive stating that personnel who had been accepted into a college had a better chance for early discharge. Bud wrote to Stuhldreher, the Wisconsin coach. Stuhldreher wrote back, verifying that Bud had been accepted at Wisconsin.

"I took the letter to my commanding officer," he said. "He threw it back across the desk at me. He said he didn't like people who tried to get out early . . . I told him I didn't think they'd miss the guy who racked the pool balls. He got upset with me, but I was persistent . . . and I had the letter."

And he had his discharge.

Bud rode a train from San Francisco to St. Louis, then hitchhiked to Superior.

The sailor was home.

"I had a mustache," he recalled. "My mother didn't say anything, but she kept looking at it. I shaved it off the next day."

A month later, he was back on the football field, practicing twice a day.

But not at Wisconsin.

4

Minnesota

The University of Minnesota is not without its legendary athletes.

Bruce Smith, All-American was the title of a movie and the name of a Golden Gopher football player of heroic stature. Nagurski and Nomellini made the Memorial Stadium turf tremble with their might, and later on, the vastly talented Bobby Bell, perhaps the greatest Gopher of all.

Basketball, too . . . Whitey Skoog excelled and Lou Hudson . . . Kevin McHale still does, with the pros.

The New York Yankees' Dave Winfield used to roam the Minnesota baseball outfield.

But the most versatile athlete in Minnesota history was a lean, solemn-faced youth from neighboring Wisconsin.

Bud Grant, the nineteen-year-old navy veteran, first had to sort out where he would go to college. Once that was done, he went on to win nine varsity letters in three sports . . . a key regular in football, basketball, and baseball . . . and he did it in less than four years.

But first there was that sorting out.

Grant had been recruited by Iowa, Minnesota, Northwestern, Notre Dame, and Wisconsin.

But the navy changed his need for attending a far-off campus.

"Going into service, especially right out of high school, made you grow up quick. When you are thrown abruptly into the company of men, it speeds up your maturing process.

"Going away to school had sounded exciting, but I traveled a lot in service," said Grant. "When I got back, the idea of staying close to home appealed to me."

And the navy changed his thinking on Notre Dame.

"I had been very much aware of Notre Dame while I was in high school," said Bud. "If you liked sports, Notre Dame was it . . . the

33

stories of Rockne and Gipp, the great tradition. I used to dream about going there and playing all the sports."

But the glamour waned when Seaman Grant visited South Bend with the Great Lakes basketball team. The dorms he saw looked like navy barracks, and the segregated climate of an all-male school likewise reminded him of the service.

Iowa and Northwestern never were serious considerations, although a wealthy Iowa alum entertained Bud in Los Angeles while he was stationed on the West Coast with the navy. "He took me to Ciro's," said Grant. "I was amazed . . . I couldn't imagine that having dinner could ever be that fancy."

That left Minnesota and Wisconsin.

Location favored Minnesota. Madison is 350 miles from Superior, Minneapolis–St. Paul is 150.

But Wisconsin offered a handsome package.

As a Badger, Bud would receive $100 a month, free use of a car for as long as he kept his studies up, and a part-time job. As a veteran, he already qualified for tuition, books, and $75 a month from the government.

"This was 1946," Grant pointed out. "I mean, I thought this was really something."

Turned out, it was too good.

Minnesota offered him, to use Bud's word, "zip."

Nothing?

Nothing.

Then why did you go to Minnesota?

To understand, it helps to remember Grant for what he was, an athlete. He didn't want the tag of "football player" or "basketball player" or "baseball player." He enjoyed all of them, and he wanted to be able to turn to each in its season. Best to remember Grant, also, for what he is, a man who does what he wants to do.

The man grew from the boy.

"Minnesota offered me nothing in the way of inducements, but there was another side to that," said Grant. "If they gave me nothing, they had no hold on me. I could do what I wanted to do. If I went to Wisconsin, on their terms, and wanted to play baseball, they could say football was paying my way, and I had to play spring football.

"I liked the idea of not owing anybody."

And the nineteen-year-old called his own shots.

"I found out later that recruiters would call my dad and ask him what I was going to do. He'd tell them, 'Don't ask me, ask the kid.'

"My parents were interested in me, but they didn't interfere with my decisions."

Grant called Stuhldreher, the Wisconsin coach, to tell him he had decided to attend Minnesota.

And if the conversation sounds similar to one that took place nearly forty years later, then you've been paying attention.

"I went over my reasons," said Bud. "I explained to him as best I could. I told him I didn't want anything more from Wisconsin, I just thought Minnesota made more sense for me. Coach Stuhldreher wanted to keep it open . . . he asked me to think about it some more and call him back the next day. I told him I appreciated everything he'd done for me, but calling back the next day wouldn't change anything, I was going to Minnesota."

And so he did.

Bud's maternal grandparents drove him to Minneapolis in August, depositing him and his suitcase at the front steps of Cooke Hall, the University of Minnesota athletic department.

A young reporter climbed the Cooke Hall steps along with Grant. The reporter was beginning his first day on the Gopher beat for the Minneapolis *Times*.

"He was the first person I met there," said Bud. "We were walking in together, and he introduced himself."

The reporter was Sid Hartman.

Like the fellow said, their relationship may have been unusual, but at least it was long.

But Sid will come back to us in these pages . . . frequently.

Bernie Bierman coached Minnesota football during Grant's years.

"Coached" seems a shallow word for it . . . Bierman was the monarch of Minnesota football.

"When I was a high school senior, I visited the university on a recruiting weekend," Bud recalled. "That was the first time I met Bernie. When it came time to go see him, I can't remember who was more nervous, me or the recruiter who was showing me around. The fellow just looked at me, and he said in this hushed, practically reverent voice, 'We're going to see Bernie now.'

"Bernie's office window faced north, I remember that . . . it was always dark. It wasn't a cheery place, and I don't think it was supposed to be. He said all the right things, I'm sure, but I didn't go to Minnesota because of Bernie Bierman. I came to respect him . . . to love him . . . but he didn't recruit me."

Who did, then?

"Nobody . . . I made my own decision."

What was Bud's impression of Bierman?

"One of power . . . Bernie was a big man, impressive in the physical sense, and he had an officer's bearing. Bernie carried authority with his presence."

What was he like?

"He wasn't comfortable, at that time, in one-on-one relationships. He spoke to the group, but he didn't often speak to you individually.

When he did, it was disconcerting, because he would ask a question and be nodding yes or no to your answer before you ever got it out.

"As a player, you never got to know Bernie until your career was over. That was when you could appreciate him, because you were a survivor.

"You'd learn, for example," said Grant, "that he was a staunch defender of every player on the squad. If you think of it, with faculty and the press and all the scrapes a young fellow can get into, it had to keep him busy. But he was totally loyal to his players."

Bierman retired to San Diego, and when the Vikings played there, he would go to the games.

"He'd come to the tunnel outside the dressing room. but he wouldn't go inside," said Bud. "He didn't feel he belonged there. So I'd go out in the hall, before a game, and we'd visit. I know that he thoroughly enjoyed the fact that I was coaching.

"The last time we met, he reminded me of a quote of his Dick Cullum had reported years before in the newspaper. Cullum quoted Bernie as saying Grant was the only player he'd coached who had never made a mistake in a game." Grant paused. "Of course, I don't know if Bernie ever really said that, but he remembered the article."

Minnesota, the school that had offered Grant nothing in the way of inducements, promptly made good on its word.

Bud had gone to school assured he would be assigned housing, but when he arrived, he learned dorm space was in short supply. Since in-state students got preference, Grant drew makeshift quarters on the third floor of the old North Tower of Memorial Stadium.

"Very high ceilings," said Bud. "I think the light cords hung down twenty-five feet from the ceiling, and there would be a twenty-five watt bulb. You could barely see. The windows had to be twenty feet up off the floor, and they were just slots in the concrete, about a foot wide. I lived there two quarters."

Grant augmented his $75 monthly check from the government by working part-time at Investors Syndicate, forerunner of Investors Diversified Services (IDS). He was a handyman.

"If they needed a desk brought up from the storeroom, I brought it up. And I cleaned up. I worked about twelve hours a week . . . I made $75 a month."

Did he consider his circumstances less than grand?

"That never occurred to me. I'd always worked. I never had an allowance as a youngster, I had a job . . . I worked in ships and coalyards . . . I never doubted that I could make my own way."

Survival was under control, but the cheerless conditions at North Tower began to wear thin.

"I was walking home from the library one night . . . you had to walk clear around the stadium to get to the tower, and the snow was over my shoe tops. I remember thinking, 'This is it . . . I've got to get out of there.' "

He did so by taking a wildly out-of-character step . . . he joined a fraternity.

Phi Delta Theta.

And, not to make him feel out of place, the Phi Delts of those years had a house almost as ancient as North Tower. The brothers were delighted to enlist a clutch of athletes lusting to escape North Tower. Along with Grant, they got Bye, the teammate from Great Lakes, Gordie Soltau, Ev Faunce, and Marv Hein.

But they got Grant on his terms.

"I told them I wasn't interested in going through initiation or that pledge stuff," said Bud. "I'd had my initiation in the navy. I didn't go to meetings . . . I'd get fined fifty cents for missing, and that was that."

Since he also didn't haze new pledges, didn't go to parties, and didn't go to dances, what did Grant do as a fraternity man?

"Played cards and was a good fellow around the house," he said.

And he liked it. The food was good, the house, though old, was an improvement on North Tower, and he was among friends. "Not all of the athletes were like me," Bud added. "Gordie Soltau ended up being president of the house."

Grant roomed with Bye, a pairing that would last through four years at the university. Years later, before Bud came back to Minnesota from Winnipeg, Bye worked for the Vikings for a time.

By the middle of his freshman year, Grant was a starter at end for the Gophers.

"We had a lot of men coming back from service on the team in 1946," said Grant. "Some of them had been away three or four years. For the most part, they didn't return to football successfully. Having been away for several years . . . and these were fellows who had been shot at in the war . . . they came back with different priorities. The older players started through the early part of the season, but we weren't doing too well. Bernie must have decided to see what the young people could do, because we started playing. We won our last three or four games."

Gopher basketball brought Bud into contact with a coach who, like Paul Brown, would impact on his future.

To make a point, however, he learned from every coach he played under . . . good lessons, as well as bad. "You can learn what not to do just as well as you can learn what to do," he said.

The Minnesota basketball coach was Dave MacMillan. "I learned more about handling people from Dave than I have from anybody else," said Grant.

"He had respect for everybody on the team, and that was a new experience for me. I'd been used to being on teams where the best players always commanded the most respect. That wasn't Mac's way . . . he had as much respect for the last sub as he did for the star of the team. That made an impression on me . . . he believed everybody was important, and he let you know that."

MacMillan's Scottish burr kept him from pronouncing Grant's nickname properly. "He called me 'Bood.' "

When Bud was named coach at Winnipeg in 1957, he stopped to see MacMillan before heading north.

"He told me two things," Bud recalled. "He said, Never chew a player out in front of his teammates, because you'll only embarrass him, and he won't listen to what you're saying. He also told me that if I had to correct a player, to always find something positive to say to him first. That way, he said, I would have the player's attention."

MacMillan coached the Gopher cagers through Bud's freshman and sophomore years.

"I was the captain when I was a sophomore," said Grant. "One game, Mac was sick, and he knew he wouldn't be able to coach. We didn't have an assistant coach . . . the only other person associated with the team was Lloyd Stein, the trainer. Mac told the press Lloyd would handle the team in the game, but he called Lloyd and me aside. He said, 'Lloyd, you're the designated coach, but, Bood, you make the substitutions, and you do what has to be done.'

"We were the only ones who knew," said Grant. "The game was a big story . . . the team coached by the trainer for a night. And Lloyd loved it . . . every time out, he'd jump up on the floor and hitch up his pants and talk. Then I'd tell the other players what we were supposed to do.

"Needless to say," Grant added, "I played the whole game."

Grant was very fond of MacMillan.

Basketball practice often forced Bud to miss dinner at the fraternity . . . he'd eat on his own, at a diner.

"Every once in a while, Mac would slip me five dollars and say, 'Bood, make sure you get a good meal tonight.'

"If Dave MacMillan lacked anything as a coach, it was toughness," said Bud. "But the qualities he did have were very special."

Grant played baseball in the spring to conclude a freshman year where he was a regular in three different sports. MacMillan coached the baseball team that year, as well. Bud played outfield. He wasn't a starter at the beginning of the season, but he ended up as the Gophers' leading hitter.

He has theories on the three sports he played.

"Football was boring to practice, the games were the attraction. Baseball's more fun to practice . . . once the game starts, you spend most of the time standing around. Basketball gave you the best of both, fun to practice and fun to play."

Miami Dolphins coach Don Shula once spoke of a secret desire to be a major league baseball manager. Grant feels he could have been a pro basketball coach.

"Basketball made sense to me," said Bud. "So much of what you do involves positioning, being aware of angles and distances. You might be in one spot, trying to defend a man, where if you were to move yourself just a foot away, to a slightly different location, it would make you so much more effective. I could see that. A lot of players go out there and do the same thing, over and over again, never aware that they're doing it wrong."

He does not share Shula's enthusiasm for directing a baseball team.

"It's kind of like bowling," said Grant. "There are only so many situations you can encounter, and you know every one of them has been encountered before. Football and basketball aren't nearly as structured as baseball . . . anything can happen. To me, that's a lot of their appeal."

The original Grant premise . . . go to Minnesota and be your own man . . . did not go unchallenged by Bierman.

"He'd never say anything to me directly," said Bud, "but he'd get his message across. Maybe an assistant coach . . . someone . . . would say, 'Look, Bernie really would like it if you'd come out for spring football.' "

Of course, Grant didn't . . . he played baseball. And every fall, when football practice began, he was listed on the fourth string of the varsity depth chart.

"Even when I was a senior. But I understood, it was Bernie's way of letting me know who was in charge. I don't blame him. The other guys had been there in the spring when I wasn't."

Bernie Bierman's football philosophy was as hard as lake ice in February: The game was an ordeal, and there was no place for weakness.

"He taught survival," said Bud. "If you survived, you played. If you didn't survive, you didn't play.

"We practiced twice a day in August, we wore these old wool uniforms that sucked the moisture right out of you. Heat, harassment, and three-hour practices . . . and never a drop of water on the field. A lot of players couldn't handle that . . . we had people with ability who didn't make it because they couldn't survive."

Bierman's austere approach didn't even permit water on the field during a game. "We've learned, since then, that water doesn't hinder performance, it helps it," said Grant. "But no one knew that in those days. I'll always remember how shocked I was, walking into the Laker locker room at halftime of my first game with them. George Mikan flopped down on a bench and absolutely guzzled two bottles of orange pop. I mean, he just poured them down his throat. I was flabbergasted."

Did Mikan change Bud's ways? He grinned. "I got to where I'd take a few swallows of pop at halftime."

For the survivors of Bierman's forced march, there was a special feeling. "Looking back, he demanded survival, but he taught us the pride that goes along with survival. If you played football for Bernie and stuck with it, you felt superior."

Bierman was a "method" coach.

"I got to where I recognized what he was doing," said Bud. "We might run a play exactly right, but if Bernie's schedule said it was time for him to make a show of getting upset, then he'd get upset and have everybody run a lap. I didn't agree with that."

There are those who will tell you that Grant didn't buy a fair amount of whatever it was Bierman might be selling at a given moment.

Bud's response to that charge?

"There were some things I didn't do with a lot of enthusiasm if I didn't believe in them."

Indeed, Grant learned some things not to do from the coach they called the Gray Eagle.

"To do something over and over again, even after you have it down pat, doesn't make sense to me. I'd rather conserve energy against the time when you'll really need it. When I pitched baseball, I threw only as many warmup pitches as I needed. Once I knew I was throwing as hard as I could with accuracy, and when I knew my curve was breaking, I stopped. I didn't want to waste one pitch in the bullpen. I think the same thing applies in coaching. In the pros, you have players who have been in your system for four, five years, some of them for ten years. They know the plays. Why have them waste effort and risk getting sloppy by practicing them too much? I'd rather conserve their strength and enthusiasm for the game, when they'll need it."

Bud Grant never played a college football or basketball game at home before less than a sellout crowd. That high level of fan interest . . . coupled with one of the more traditional rites of college athletes . . . helped augment Grant's slender budget and permitted him to pay off a couple of bank notes incurred by the purchase of lake property in Wisconsin.

He scalped tickets.

"Players got complimentary tickets and an option to purchase additional tickets," said Grant. "As a freshman, it was two comps and two options, as a sophomore it was four and four, and as a junior and senior it was six and six. They'd bring about twenty-five dollars each," said Grant. Bud bought up tickets other players didn't use . . . he paid $15 for the comps and $10 for options. By the time he was a senior, he had a bustling ticket business. The worst part of the venture had to do with timing . . . occasionally Bud found himself having to deliver tickets on Friday nights before Gopher home games.

Today, in line with the "Do as I say not as I do" policy, one of Grant's pet peeves as a coach is for his players to be in the ticket business.

"I implore our players to get rid of their tickets early," he said. "I didn't like having to think about tickets the night before a game, and I don't want them doing it. I tell them, 'If you're going to be on this team, don't ever let me see you fooling around with tickets on the day of a game.' "

MacMillan was replaced as Minnesota basketball coach after Bud's second year. His replacement was Ozzie Cowles. Introducing Ozzie hot on the heels of a ticket-scalping story wasn't planned, but it's appropriate.

"Ozzie," Grant recalled, "was a very unusual guy. He was a good basketball coach, quite innovative, but he was a real departure from Dave MacMillan.

"When we'd go on the road for a game, we'd all eat together. We might go into a restaurant, and Ozzie would have the starters sit with him at a table, but rather than have the reserves sit at a table next to us, he'd get them over on the other side of the room. Then he'd order steak for us and veal cutlet for the reserves. Once, at Purdue, we slept in the student infirmary, on cots."

It was pointed out to Grant that Purdue had a fine student union that was, in fact, a hotel.

"I know! We stayed there in football. But Ozzie had us on cots when we went there for basketball. He had a way of economizing with the expense money."

But a trip to Michigan during Grant's junior year provided the most memorable Ozzie Cowles story.

"Players could get a ticket or two for a road game from Ozzie, but the circumstances had to be pretty spectacular. Otherwise, he sold the tickets . . . rather, he had our student manager sell them . . . and pocketed the dough."

The Gophers went to play at Michigan, and tickets were at a premium. Adding to the plot, Cowles had left the Michigan coaching job to go to Minnesota. As soon as they arrived at the Michigan fieldhouse, Cowles sent student manager Bob Casey out into the lobby to sell tickets.

The Michigan arena had poor lighting, and when the Gopher players returned to the dressing room after warmups, each man found a pair of dark glasses in his locker.

"Ozzie was very proud of that," said Bud. "He told us to wear the dark glasses while we waited to go back out. He said it would make the lights in the arena seem brighter."

Grant and his teammates donned their dark glasses, and student manager Casey came in for a whispered conversation with Cowles. "Ozzie was upset," said Bud. "It was something about not getting rid of the tickets at the right price." Cowles and Casey left the dressing room.

The cause for Cowles's upset was waiting in the lobby—in the form of a police officer, who announced his intention of arresting Cowles and Casey as scalpers. Ozzie told the cop he couldn't be arrested, since he was the Minnesota coach, but the cop didn't believe him. Fortunately, just as he was about to be hauled away, a Michigan official intervened.

"We were still waiting in the dressing room, wearing our dark glasses," said Bud. "We had no idea where Ozzie had gone. Finally, one of the officials came to the door and said it was time to go out. Then he saw all of us, in our dark glasses, and that really pulled him up short. He asked where Ozzie was, and we said we didn't know. He just shook his head and said we'd better come out. We were walking onto the court when Ozzie came back."

No dark glasses at Iowa, but Grant's basketball visits there lighted the fuse of a powderkeg that kept things lively for two seasons.

"I was a sophomore, and I was moving on defense past their big man, Noble Jorgenson. I suppose the official was looking the other way, because when I went by Jorgenson I hit him in the chest with a left hook . . . I was paying him back for the elbows to the head I'd been getting. It staggered him because he hadn't seen me, and I gave him a pretty good shot.

"But because I was on the move, I was past him before he knew who had slugged him. He looked around, and the closest Minnesota player he saw was Bill Pepper, who had just come into the game and had nothing to do with what I'd done.

"Well, Jorgenson hit Bill Pepper with a haymaker and broke his jaw.

"The next year, when we went to Iowa, the floor was ringed with football players wearing their Iowa letter sweaters. We knew why they were there," said Grant.

The "why" wasn't long in developing. A bump led to pushing led to a brawl. The football players grabbed the Minnesota basketball players and began to rough them up.

Did Grant get grabbed?

"Not for very long." The Iowa band played the national anthem to get that donnybrook sorted out. The governor of Minnesota, according to Grant, demanded an apology of his Iowa counterpart after that incident and said that without assurance of future peace, Minnesota would not play at Iowa again.

Bud played offensive and defensive end for the Gopher football team. "We were single wing," said Grant, "so we ran more than we threw, but I made some catches."

He made enough that Bierman called him the most sure-handed receiver he'd ever seen.

One thing that set Grant's receptions apart was his penchant for lateraling the ball to a teammate after the catch, if he saw he was going to be tackled.

"I'd tell players, 'Come to me if I make a catch, because I'll be looking to lateral to you.' I think we got three or four touchdowns that way.

"I remember one catch . . . I knew I was going to get hit, so I looked around for someone to dump the ball off to. The closest guy to me was Leo Nomellini [a huge lineman who went on to become a great pro at San Francisco]. Leo was pounding along, hollering 'Bud . . . Bud!' I tossed the ball to him. I think he had a 10-yard lead on the nearest defender when he got the ball, but they caught him after he'd gone 20 yards . . . he was dragging four or five people, snorting like a locomotive."

Dick Siebert took over as Minnesota baseball coach when MacMillan retired . . . he was fresh from a pro career at Philadelphia.

"I learned a lot about baseball from him," said Grant. "I was an outfielder, but I think I followed him around. If he talked to the pitchers, I listened. If he talked to the infielders, I listened. He knew the game, and he could communicate what he knew."

Interesting, in retrospect, to consider the coaches he played under at Minnesota.

Bierman, the legendary figure, bleak and demanding, but curiously limited at close range. Almost regal, but uncomfortable in simple one-to-one communication. Insulated.

MacMillan, the softie. Not a driver, but a fine coach. And overwhelmingly a people person.

Cowles . . . innovative and a bold thinker, and a rogue.

Siebert, giving off the whiff of the true professional, a specialist in a sport.

Grant took from all of them, although his memory of going to Bierman for coaching advice prompted a smile.

"I talked to Bernie before I started coaching at Winnipeg. I asked him if there was anything he could tell me that I should know. We had a nice visit, but I can't think of one thing I got out of it. He had trouble with that, the one-on-one. And I think I am no different than a lot of other people who played for Bernie . . . you hated him when you started out, but you loved him when you finished."

Grant was twice an All-Big Nine selection in football and won most valuable player awards in both basketball and football.

Do any memories stand out?

"It's funny," he said, "but I don't really remember things until people remind me of them. I guess they're in storage. I'll meet someone, and they might say, 'Oh, I'll never forget that play you made against . . .' And they'll recall it in detail. When that happens, when someone reminds me, then I remember. But there have been a lot of games."

One was against Washington, to begin the 1949 season, Grant's last at Minnesota. Hugh McElhenny, the Hall of Fame running back, returned the opening kickoff for a touchdown for the Huskies. Minnesota, however, went on to win the game.

And Grant took a deep breath, and pulled off a caper that would have turned the Gray Eagle white, had he known of it.

During the week, before the Washington game, Bud had had a call from a fellow over in Ridgeland, Wisconsin. Seems Ridgeland's town baseball team had a grudge game coming up Sunday, and the fellow was wondering if Grant might be available to pitch. Bud spent his summers pitching town baseball in Wisconsin and Minnesota. He had a reputation.

Grant told the fellow from Ridgeland he was playing football . . . said his baseball season was over.

"He said he knew that," Grant recalled, "but they really wanted me to come over because this was a grudge game. He said they'd give me seventy-five dollars to pitch."

You are safe in your assumption that collegiate football players are not encouraged to pitch baseball for money during the football season.

Grant told this story, sitting in his Vikings office. He paused for a time, watching a song sparrow flit about in a bush outside his window.

"If they'd offered fifty dollars, which was what I got for most games, I probably wouldn't have done it."

The sparrow flew away.

Grant shook his head, and his face almost mirrored the pain of nearly forty years ago.

"You can't imagine," he said, "what it's like to pick up a baseball and pitch a game, the day after you've played a football game. I was so stiff, I could hardly get out of bed Sunday morning. But I drove over to Ridgeland . . . I tried not to think of what would happen if Bernie found out. I pitched, we won, and everybody in Ridgeland was happy. But my arm felt like it was going to drop off."

Summer baseball was a Grant staple, through his years at the university and while he was a pro player. He pitched most for Osceola, Wisconsin, but "over the years, there weren't too many towns in western Wisconsin and Minnesota that I didn't play in."

The town teams took their baseball seriously. "There was a lot of pride and local interest," Bud said. Feelings ran high . . . which meant there was some wagering on the games. If he pitched, Grant got paid fifty dollars . . . if he didn't pitch, he didn't get paid.

"I'd go into a town, and if the situation looked right, I'd tell the fellow who hired me to pitch that I'd go double or nothing. That meant he had to lay off the money he was going to pay me in bets. If we won, I doubled, if we lost, I got nothing. Of course, I picked my spots."

The move from football to basketball didn't happen in 1949, Grant's senior year at Minnesota.

"When Ozzie Cowles replaced MacMillan the year before, things changed a lot," said Grant. "Ozzie got rid of some of the players from Dave's team. I still played, but it wasn't as much fun."

As the football season wound down and basketball workouts began, Grant read an article where Cowles wondered publicly if Bud would be able to get his basketball legs back. "It left me with some doubts about what the basketball season might hold for me," said Grant.

Remember Sid Hartman, the young sports writer whom Grant had met on his first day at the university?

If you are not of the Twin Cities or an occasional visitor, "Hartman's Roundup" probably has escaped your attention. And for a sports junkie, that's too bad, because Sid's column, over the several decades, has fairly bristled with notes and quotes, a kind of ratta-tat-tat chronicle of comings and goings, ups and downs, and ins and outs of the local and national sports scenes. It's the same principle as the daily NYSE summary, only an easier read.

Some years ago, an airborne posse of Midwest sports writers was touring Big Ten football camps during the preseason.

Legend has it that, as the charter flight came on approach to Minneapolis–St. Paul airport, one travel-weary scribe turned to his seatmate and said, "What stop is this, I can't remember."

"Minnesota," the seatmate advised him.

"Can't be," growled the weary one. "If it was, Hartman would be out on the wing by now, taking notes."

Sid, for his part, has never presented himself as a serious threat to that common journalistic flower that regards itself as being pretty darned literate.

"If people wanna read *War and Peace,* they'll go to the library," Sid once counseled this penman . . . at a time, it should be noted, when he was my boss. "Just tell the story, okay? I give 'em quotes and short pieces they can read in a hurry . . . they like that."

"They" must, because they've been reading Sid for a long, long time.

"Sid," said Grant, "works harder at what he does than anybody I've ever been around."

The point of all this is that at the time in question, the winter of 1949, Sid was working hard at not one job but two.

In addition to demonstrating a news-gathering zeal to make the CIA envious, Sid ran the Minneapolis Laker basketball team.

In the event these pages are read by any basketball fan in his or her midtwenties, it should be pointed out that the Lakers were big, long before Kareem and Magic.

But not in Los Angeles.

At the time Bud Grant was puzzling his future, or lack of it, with the Gopher basketball team, the Lakers were the reigning power of the NBA, playing in Minneapolis and owned by Max Winter . . . the same Max Winter who later moved on to ownership of the Vikings.

Max and Sid were friends.

"Max was the visible control," said Bud, "he went to the league meetings, and the public thought of Max when they thought of the Lakers. . . .

"But Sid ran the team."

You mean, Sid helped out some?

"I mean Sid ran the operation, lock, stock, and barrel. He negotiated contracts, signed players, and ran the club," said Grant.

And because of an injury, the Lakers needed a player.

Sid told Grant there was an opening. Bud said he didn't know how the pros and the colleges operated in those days, but he was petitioned through. "There wasn't really a lot of talk," said Grant, "it just seemed like a good opportunity. By Christmas, I was playing in the NBA."

Grant was asked if he ever thought of it as unusual, his trekking from one sport to another, through high school, the service, and college.

"It never entered my mind. I never thought of moving from one sport to the other as a burden or as anything out of the ordinary. I enjoyed what I was doing."

Did he ever . . . the next question went . . . lack for confidence during the ascent from schoolboy athletics to service to college, and on into the pros?

Did you ever wonder if you were good enough?

Grant grinned.

"Nope . . . and there was a time when I thought I probably could have been the heavyweight boxing champ, too. Not Marciano . . . I wouldn't have wanted any part of him . . . but I think I could have handled Patterson."

5

Pro

This wasn't your standard transition from college athlete to professional. . . .

Which, come to think of it, seems to slot it neatly into the stream of Grant's progression through life.

On the one hand, you had Bud leaving school early, and long before terms like "coming out" and "hardship" had become a part of the sports lexicon.

On the other, you had Sid Hartman, the moonlighting reporter, putting the deal together.

Providing a third hand is available, you had Grant playing the "wrong" sport.

Bud was a good basketball player . . . strong defense, good rebounder, and he could run all night . . . but he remained a 6-foot-3 forward in a sport dominated by big men, and not a prolific scorer.

He signed with the Lakers for $3,500 . . . contract, not bonus. George Mikan, the great center, was the club's highest paid player at $33,000 a year.

Did he feel like his football days were behind him?

"At that age, I don't know that your long-range planning is really into effect yet. When you're coming out of college, you're about as broke as you're ever going to be in your entire life. The Lakers represented a chance to make some money . . . it wasn't much, but it certainly wasn't the worst."

The money wasn't the only thing different in pro sports at the time . . . Grant spoke to the difference in the men who played the game.

"The thing was, you could do other things that would pay at least as well as professional sport," he said. "Which meant the people who played, very often, were really dedicated . . . they wanted to play.

"They played because it was important to them.

"Today, you have players who can't afford not to play. They're not

49

sure playing is their first choice, but they know it's their best choice in terms of generating maximum dollars within a fairly short period of time.

"This has been said a lot of different ways, but it's really true . . . today, you have fellows playing who have had enough football. They've been in organized football from Little Leagues on up the ladder. Some of them are no longer enamored with playing, with making the sacrifices and doing the things you have to do for a team.

"I'm not talking about all players, I'm talking about some. They hang on as long as they can, but it still doesn't change what's in their hearts. They're not playing because they love the sport."

In Grant's time, it wasn't unusual for an athlete to leave the pro ranks in his prime or to forgo it completely.

"Clayt Tonnemaker [a football teammate at Minnesota] was an example," said Bud. "He was a great linebacker for the Packers, and he walked away from it in the prime of his career. He recognized that there was going to be a life beyond football and the sooner he got there, the better. He ended up with a fine career in business."

Were athletic careers shorter in Grant's day?

"They might have been. It wasn't a year-round job. There was the old stereotype of the pro football player coming into training camp fat and out of shape. We don't see that anymore. The players today are paid at a level where they don't have to work a second job during the off-season . . . and because they know their body is their meal ticket, they spend that time conditioning themselves. And there's less tendency now to leave early for that career opportunity."

Did Bud ever envision a career away from sport?

"Not really. For a time, I had thoughts about running a fishing resort, but I've been in sports all my life. And I've enjoyed every aspect of my involvement. And I've been involved. In football, I played every position, over the years, except center, guard, and tackle.

"I'm not talking about practicing at a position, I'm talking about starting and playing a game."

He was not so broadly involved in professional basketball . . . Bud was a "spot" player, with no illusions and no regrets.

"I liked basketball. You know, there's a lot more to it than people think. It looks pretty simple, people running up and down a court, but it's more than that.

"I wasn't a great basketball player," said Grant. "I played on a great team, and there were times I was able to contribute to our success."

Grant was a small forward, whose strengths were defense and mobility. "I could match up with a guy up to 6-foot-6, but after that, I had a problem."

The Lakers won the NBA championship in 1949–50. During that

basketball season, Grant was made a first-round selection in the National Football League player draft by the Philadelphia Eagles. At about the time of that draft, he was having one of his moments as a "spot" player for the Lakers.

"We were at Syracuse in the playoff series," Bud recalled. "We hadn't won there, and they hadn't won in Minneapolis. We were down by two points with less than a minute to play. We had the ball, and the play we had on was for Jim Pollard to come around a pick and take the shot."

Grant was in the game because a starter was in foul trouble, but he wasn't supposed to take the shot.

"But when Pollard came off the pick, he threw the ball to me. You talk about surprised . . . the only thing I knew was time was running out. I just put the ball up, and it went in. John Kundla was our coach, and he had ulcers . . . I don't think that play gave him any relief."

With ten seconds remaining in the game, Syracuse had a last chance . . . only the shot was blocked by Grant, who flipped the ball to Bob Harrison. Harrison scored as time ran out, and the Lakers evened the playoff series, going on to win.

"At that point, it was the most important game of our season," said Grant. "We got a kick out of the fact that it was Harrison and Grant, not Mikan and Pollard, who won the game."

In his second Laker season, Bud's last-second basket defeated the Boston Celtics, ensuring the Lakers the regular season championship and home-court advantage for the playoffs.

"My 'moments' were few and far between," said Grant, "but I was able to make a contribution."

Though he was playing basketball, football was not wholly removed from the picture. Bud talked to officials of the Philadelphia Eagles in the spring of 1950.

"There was me and four of them in a Philadelphia hotel room," Grant recalled. "They offered me a $7,500 contract, no bonus, and nothing guaranteed. I had been the twelfth player selected in the NFL draft, and I told them I thought that should mean something. They said it meant I could sign for $7,500."

With his salary and playoff money, Bud had made $6,000 playing basketball. He also was living where he wanted to live. When the Lakers offered him a $500 increase for the 1950–51 season, and with the chance for playoff money looking good again, Grant told the Eagles he wasn't interested.

He had been selected to play in the College All-Star football game in the summer of 1950, but declined the invitation.

Not to spring Pat Grant as a total surprise . . . because her role, in her words, comes later . . . but the reason Grant didn't play in the All-Star game was that he got married that day.

It has been suggested that professional basketball, with its many games, the bruising tempo of play, and a travel schedule nigh onto impossible, is the most demanding of sports.

Grant's Laker memories do nothing to dispel that theory.

"We flew on DC3s," said Bud, "and I remember two things most clearly. One was I marveled at how the big men could ever get any rest in those little cramped seats. It was tough enough for a guy my size, let alone somebody huge, like Mikan. But they had to do it . . . it wasn't unusual for us to play a Saturday night game in Boston or New York and then play on Sunday afternoon in Minneapolis. By DC3, that was six or seven hours, depending on the head winds. Those big guys would curl up somehow . . . they sort of wrapped themselves in and out of a row of seats . . . and they'd sleep. Hard as they played, they had to."

The second recollection was of the flights themselves.

"A DC3 wasn't designed to fly over weather, it was designed to fly through it," said Grant. "There were times, when the storms really got bad, that the praying was loud enough so you could hear it."

George Mikan, the giant DePaul All-American, became one of pro basketball's premier big men with the Lakers. He holds a special place in Bud Grant's memories.

"He was the greatest competitor, for any sport, I ever played with," said Bud.

"He'd just keep pounding up and down the court, taking all the abuse the other teams could give him. Some tall men are slender, their feet hardly touch the floor . . . but George was big, big everywhere. When he went up and down the floor, you heard it. Every team we played would double- or triple-team him and put its hatchet men on him. In those days, the pros didn't have a rule against zone defenses.

"We'd throw the ball into the pivot, and everybody would jump on George.

"There were times when George would sit down on the bench during a time-out . . . he'd just be covered with welts and bruises from fists and elbows and knees . . . and I'd wonder if he could even stand up again. But he would . . . and he'd go back out there and play like a demon. He was the toughest man I ever played with in anything, I bar none."

The NBA had two kinds of days, game and travel.

"Once the season started, we hardly ever practiced," said Bud.

John Kundla, who went on to coach at the University of Minnesota, was the Laker coach during Bud's two seasons with the club. Like Grant, Kundla had been a disciple of Gopher coach Dave Mac-Millan.

"What Kundla did for us was keep us together," said Bud. "And that isn't an easy thing to do. When you think of the length of the season, the travel, coping with the success of the team, it took a special kind of person to keep everybody on the same page."

For Grant, off-days on the road consisted of a lot of gin rummy and a modest amount of reading.

"The gin lessons were expensive," he pointed out. "If I read something, I'm interested in learning. I don't enjoy fiction, because I have less interest in learning what might be in somebody's imagination. I'm not especially interested in politics, but I can enjoy reading about situations in politics . . . how they were arrived at and how they were dealt with."

If Mikan's guzzling orange pop at halftime came as a shock to Grant, a product of Bierman's cloistered training rules, it was nothing compared to seeing players smoke in the locker room at halftime of a game. "And I don't mean just one cigarette . . . they'd smoke right through the half.

"That went against anything I've ever learned, and I don't endorse it. There probably isn't anything I take a stronger stand against than smoking. I'll do anything I can to thwart it. But I didn't see it have any effect on the players on our Laker team, at least not short-term."

After the season ended, the Lakers would barnstorm throughout the Dakotas, Iowa, Minnesota, and Wisconsin. "We played twenty-eight games, as I recall," said Bud. "We got paid $25 a game." One such tour ended in Grand Forks, North Dakota, on a Saturday night. Grant pitched a baseball game in Spring Valley, Wisconsin, on Sunday afternoon.

"My training for that summer of baseball consisted of carrying a couple gloves and a ball on the barnstorming tour," he said. "Jim Pollard would play catch with me in motel parking lots."

The first home Bud and Pat Grant purchased was a log cabin on Forest Lake, north of St. Paul.

"There was no running water, the outhouse was about forty yards back in the woods, and the fishing was excellent," said Bud. "It was a great place to live."

However, Pat Grant had memories of Forest Lake which were less enthusiastic and will be treated in a later chapter.

In fact, Pat was there, at the cabin, awaiting the birth of their first child, Kathy, in the summer of 1951. Bud wasn't . . . Bud was in the training camp of the Philadelphia Eagles and not too happy about it.

"I knew my future wasn't going to be in basketball," Grant said. "I called the Eagles again, after my second season with the Lakers.

They said they were still interested, but the price had gone down from $7,500 a year to $7,000. My discussions were with Vince McNally . . . we talked several times, but the numbers didn't change. They finally said it was take it or leave it. Pat was expecting, and I knew I'd gone as far as I was going to go in basketball. So I took it."

With the baby due shortly, Grant asked for an extension on reporting to training camp. The Eagles gave him a week.

"The baby still hadn't been born, and I got a telegram from them on the weekend. They said be there Monday or forget it." Grant was on the practice field Monday afternoon. He didn't like his contract, but he signed it . . . to Bud's thinking, that first contract was Strike One on the Eagles.

Strike Two came three days later.

Two days after Grant reported to training camp, his first child, Kathy, was born. Not knowing how to reach her husband by telephone, Pat Grant sent a telegram.

"The telegram reached camp the next evening," Bud recalled. "The PR man, a fellow named Hogan, stuck it in his pocket and carried it around with him that night and all the next day. Finally, he saw me in the dining hall that night and said, 'Hey, I've got a telegram for you.' He'd been carrying it around with him. That was Strike Two."

The Eagles put him at defensive end . . . a 6-foot-3, 200-pound defensive end.

"The first game of the regular season was against the Cardinals in Chicago," said Grant. "The starter at left defensive end went down with a knee in the first quarter. I played every down the rest of the season."

He ended up leading the team in quarterback sacks.

Bud was, by today's standards, better-sized to play defensive back than defensive line. "We played the Eagle defense, a five-man front. That meant I was split out a little wider at end . . . I was able to avoid some of the traffic on a pass-rush, but not on a run. When the other team ran a sweep, there was plenty of traffic."

One prime problem to be contended with was Marion Motley, the huge fullback of Great Lakes acquaintance, now with the Cleveland Browns.

Grant's forte as a defensive player was mobility. "I worked off people, worked around them . . . I was quick enough to slip a block. If I thought a sweep was coming, I could get off quick enough on the snap to beat the pulling guards into the backfield. I tackled Motley that way the first time we met . . . I was in the Browns' backfield before the guards could get out to meet me. I think it surprised both of us . . . at least, I know it surprised me."

The 1951 Philadelphia Eagles were a team in difficulty. They won four games and lost eight, and played under two coaches—Bo McMillin and Wayne Millner.

Did the contract problems rankle Grant through the season?

"No, I put it on the shelf and played football.

"I don't like to let something upset me," he added. "I think that feeling restricts you. I don't mean I won't lose my temper, but to just smolder over something, to be bitter and hold on to a thing you think is wrong . . . I think that's harmful. I know people who can be driving down the highway, and if someone cuts them off, they'll be mad for an hour. That's a waste. I might not like it when it happens, and I might say, 'Hey, you dummy,' but then I forget it. Maybe the guy was in a bigger hurry than I was . . . maybe he was mad about something . . . who cares? It's his problem, not mine. What good does it do to get mad and hold on to it? I wasn't happy with the way the Eagles handled my situation, but I didn't dwell on it."

One of pro football's most fabled defenders played behind Grant in the Eagle defense, linebacker Chuck Bednarik.

"We were playing the Giants, and they had us backed up, near our own goal line," said Bud. "As the Giants came out of the huddle, up to the line, Chuck hollered at me, and pointed to the space between me and the defensive tackle. He had this hoarse, scary voice.

"He hollered, 'Don't you let 'em come down inside of you, Grant! Keep 'em outta there!

"Well, they snapped the ball, and, sure enough, they blocked me outside and went right through the hole Chuck was talking about, for the touchdown. There was this huge pile of bodies in the end zone, and Bednarik was on the bottom of it. I could hear him hollering, 'Grant . . . I'm gonna kill you, Grant.' I hoped they'd never unpile . . . Chuck was a tough guy."

The season took its toll on the 200-pound defensive end.

"The day after the last game, we were packed up and ready to drive back to Minnesota," said Bud. "But we had to wait a day . . . I was so beat-up I couldn't sit in a car."

That off-season brought more basketball and baseball. Grant worked on the development of a Galloping Gophers basketball team, former university athletes who barnstormed the state much as he had done with the Lakers.

"Only the games were tougher," said Grant. "We'd play town teams, but they'd usually run in a couple of college players, guys from Concordia or Moorhead or wherever. We had former football players, fellows like Bob McNamara and Gino Cappelletti." The Galloping Gophers commanded a $150 fee, usually split six ways, with money taken out for gas.

Grant played baseball that summer for Osceola, Wisconsin, and a number of other town teams in Minnesota and Wisconsin. His fee ranged from $25 to $50 a game.

"The Northwestern Umpires Association had a newspaper that covered all the leagues, that was how you matched up with a team that needed a pitcher for a game," he said. "I suppose the word got around, everybody in those leagues knew one another."

If you may draw a parallel between country baseball and the Old West, Grant was a "hired gun" brought in to defend a town.

"I had my own pants and spikes, but I'd wear the jersey and cap of the team that hired me," he said. "I got a lot of strange fits."

Bud told a baseball story from that summer of 1951.

"I pitched a big game for Pierz, against Little Falls, in Minnesota.

"My pitching, normally, had a little show business connected to it . . . I threw a lot of junk and used different motions. I did a lot of that, because I usually pitched three times a week, and it was easier on my arm than throwing hard stuff every pitch.

"I had some tricks," Grant added. "I'd throw a couple of really wild pitches, maybe three feet behind a batter or over his cap. Then I'd watch the dugout to see who was wincing . . . that way, I knew which batters would be stepping in the bucket when they got up there. Or I'd throw hard and put the ball into the dirt, out in front of the plate . . . I'd get enough scuff marks on a ball to help my breaking pitches."

The game at Pierz against Little Falls saw a stiff wind blowing in, right at the batter. "It was more like a gale," said Bud. "And my fastball was never better. I think I struck out thirteen batters . . . I didn't need all my junk pitches."

Grant batted cleanup for Pierz and tripled and scored the only run in a 1–0 victory.

"The Pierz people were delighted . . . there had been a lot of betting on the game, and it was a real point of pride for the two towns. After the game, I remember there were horse tanks full of beer, a real celebration. I got paid 50 bucks and was getting ready to leave when the Pierz manager told me they had a game coming up against Brainerd, and they wanted me to pitch for them.

"I knew Brainerd was an independent team . . . that meant they were so good nobody wanted them in their league. They were one of the few towns that had jobs for the players and brought them in from out of town for the whole summer. Brainerd, by the standards of those days, was big-league. But they offered me 75 bucks, so I said I'd show up."

Grant drove to Brainerd on the appointed day and, as was his custom, watched the opposing team take batting practice. It was a hot, humid, perfectly still summer night . . . so still the bugs hung in swarms in the air.

"After I watched them hit, I figured there were four or five guys I could pitch to . . . the rest, I'd have to work around, because there was no way I could let them hit the ball. I knew I'd have to walk some people."

He had to walk a lot of people.

"I must have thrown 250 pitches . . . there were just too many good hitters to pitch around all of them. We got beat, 8–5."

After the game, Grant went into the dressing room to shower.

"I was the only player there," he said. "On those town teams, players would just take off after a game . . . if they won, they'd hit every bar on the way home; if they lost, they just went home. But I always wanted a shower. Over the years, I showered in filling stations, in people's houses where I didn't know the people, or with a garden hose. But I always wanted a shower.

"The Pierz manager was the only other person in the clubhouse. I was tired and hot and dry, so I asked him if he could find me a bottle of pop.

"I took a shower, and when I came out, the room was empty. I went over to the bench where my stuff was, and there was a bottle of orange pop with my $75 under it.

"That was the last contact I ever had with anybody from Pierz."

Bud went back to the Eagles for the 1952 NFL season at his rookie salary of $7,000. "I told them I thought it should count for something that I played all the time on defense and led the team in dumping the quarterback. They said they couldn't go any higher." Grant did extract one concession from the Eagles . . . they moved him from defense to offense. "I figured if individual accomplishment was what it took to get more money, I'd better play offense."

He agreed to play, but he refused to sign the contract the club had offered him.

Uncomfortable with the situation, the Eagles sent Grant to NFL Commissioner Bert Bell, whose offices were in Philadelphia.

"I had no agent, and I didn't understand all the language of the contract," said Bud. "I asked Bell what would happen if I didn't sign. He said I would be playing on my option if I didn't sign." Bell explained the option clause of a contract to Grant. One thing he learned was that, if he didn't sign, the Eagles' claim on his services would end after the 1952 season.

Bud was called in by Bell three times during the season and urged to sign.

"I told him I couldn't sign," he said. "I didn't think it was a fair contract."

Moved from defense to offense, Grant won a starting job at end, forcing the 1951 regulars, Pete Pihos and Bobby Walston, to split time on the other side. He caught fifty-seven passes, tops on the Eagles and second in the NFL. He was selected to play in the Pro Bowl.

A Grant teammate in the latter stages of his 1951 rookie season was Neill Armstrong, a swift receiver and defensive back from Oklahoma A&M. Their paths would run close to one another in the future.

Armstrong had played in the Canadian League in 1951, then returned to finish the same season with Philadelphia, since the CFL year ends early in November.

He did that just once . . . the NFL promptly made a rule prohibiting a player from playing in any other league in the same season.

Grant had been contacted by Winnipeg of the Canadian League while he was playing college football at Minnesota, and he knew several players in the CFL. During the 1952 NFL season, he contacted George Trafton, the coach at Winnipeg.

"We can't talk to you if you're under contract," said Trafton.

"What if I'm playing on my option?" Grant asked.

"Fine," said Trafton. "Play on the option."

The night the 1952 season ended, Grant reached Trafton by phone.

"I'd need ten thousand to sign with you," he said.

"You've got it," said Trafton.

The next morning, Grant went to the Eagle offices to see what they had in store for him for 1953. The answer was $8,000.

"I'd been there two seasons," said Bud. "I led the defense in sacks my first year, I led the team in pass receptions my second year. I told them I thought I was worth more than that. They said I couldn't make more than the veterans. I asked them why. The answer was, 'You just can't.' I told them I couldn't sign, and they told me if I didn't, I couldn't play in the Pro Bowl."

Strike Three.

"I told them what they could do with the Pro Bowl invitation and their contract offer. I went home and called Trafton and told him I was going to Canada."

Thus did Grant become the first NFL player to play out his option and free himself to go to another team.

Winnipeg, Manitoba, lies some fifty miles above the American border, roughly on a line marking the boundary between Minnesota and North Dakota. It is considerably more like Grant's homeland than was Philadelphia, a good deal closer, not only in count of miles, but in style of life as well. Like the Twin Cities of Minneapolis and St. Paul, it offered city life, but the country was just moments away.

Winnipeg stands at the eastern boundary of the great Canadian prairie, which stretches across Manitoba and Saskatchewan on to Alberta. It is the shipping center for prairie wheat farming. The Red River, flowing north, passes through the city en route to Lake Winnipeg. Bud Grant found himself handy to hunting and fishing, and thrust into a football network that flourished from French-speaking Montreal west to Vancouver, on the shores of the Pacific. In Canada, it was a national game.

"The games themselves, the interest in the season, the playoffs . . . football in Canada was more exciting than it had been in the States," said Bud. "Part of the problem is that, down here, we don't know a lot about the Canadian game, and we don't make an effort to learn more.

"We know they start earlier and finish up earlier because of the weather up there, and we know the field's bigger and the rules are different. But we kind of look down our noses at the Canadian game in comparison to the NFL. We minimize it.

"Believe me, to the Canadians, it was important.

"The Grey Cup, which is their Super Bowl, is a week-long celebration. The people . . . little people in the towns and people from the farms . . . would save up and find a way to get to Grey Cup. The Eastern winner plays the Western winner, and it was truly a unifying of national spirit. It was a great party . . . not unruly or a week-long drunk, but everybody just had a wonderful time. I had never been around people who know how to have a good time like Canadians do."

Trafton remained as Grant's coach at Winnipeg in 1953, but gave way to Allie Sherman in 1954, another import, who would go on to coach the New York Giants.

Bud played receiver on offense and halfback on defense . . . his wingmate on both occasions was Neill Armstrong, the former league jumper from the Eagles. Canadian teams have twelve players to a side, one more than their American counterparts. The Canadian game has just three downs, as opposed to four in this country, and the field is both longer and wider. Additionally, the CFL end zone is twenty-five yards deep, to just ten in the NFL.

"Here, the end zone is something you run through after you score," said Grant. "Up there, you played a lot of the game in the end zones."

A significant difference between the two games with regard to scoring is the "single" or "rouge" in the Canadian game . . . one point awarded for a ball kicked over the opponent's goal line and not returned.

Winnipeg posted an 8–8 record in 1953 . . . good enough for third place in the CFL West, but not good enough to keep Trafton from being replaced by Sherman.

And Grant resumed learning from negatives.

"Allie had favorites," said Bud. "And I was one of them. But if you weren't a favorite, he could really get on you. Eventually, the Canadian players on the team became alienated by him." CFL clubs were permitted twelve American imports, and made up the bulk of their roster from homegrowns.

Was there a big difference between the two?

"Really, the biggest difference was experience," said Grant. "We had some Canadians who were outstanding athletes . . . but their development level wasn't as accelerated as the Americans because they didn't have as strong a base of experience."

CFL rookie Grant caught sixty-eight passes to lead the Blue Bombers in that category, and on defense he set a CFL record, intercepting five passes in a game against Regina.

Does he remember that game?

"Just that Frank Filchock and Glenn Dobbs were the passers for Regina," said Bud. "I must have guessed right a couple times."

Just as well . . . Grant's record performance didn't make headlines in Winnipeg, anyway. Lorne Benson, a Canadian running back on the Blue Bomber squad, scored six touchdowns in the same game.

"At that time, we played sixteen games in a season that ran ten weeks," said Grant. "We played doubleheaders . . . a game on Saturday and a game on Monday. One year, with the playoffs, we played five games in fifteen days."

Bud was Winnipeg's leading receiver in each of the four seasons that he played, finishing with 216 career catches. As it had done under Trafton, Winnipeg finished third in the west in three years under Sherman. The 1956 team posted a 9–7 mark, but still finished third, and Sherman was relieved.

Grant played in the Canadian All-Star game, his third in four years, after the 1956 season. The game was played in Vancouver, and Bud was joined by five Bomber teammates—Buddy Alliston, George Druxman, Bob McNamara, Buddy Tinsley, and a spectacular rookie import, lineman Calvin Jones from Iowa.

Sherman had been relieved before Grant left for the All-Star game. Jim Russell, the Winnipeg club president, called Grant before he left for Vancouver and told him he wanted to see him upon his return.

The West All-Stars romped to a 35–0 victory over the East at Vancouver with Grant catching two touchdown passes from Frank Tripucka. It would be Grant's last game as a player. Bud and his Winnipeg teammates were scheduled to leave for home the following day, a Sunday, in the afternoon. After the game, however, they learned they could catch a Sunday morning flight.

"When it came time for us to leave the hotel that morning, we were all in the lobby except Cal. I called his room and woke him up, twice," said Grant. "The second time, he told me he wanted to sleep in and would take the afternoon flight. We told him there was time, to come on down, but he said, 'No, go on without me.' "

They did.

And the afternoon flight (with the names of Grant and McNamara listed on the passenger manifest due to an oversight) crashed, killing all passengers and crew.

The afternoon flight left Vancouver for Calgary, but was forced back promptly by bad weather. The effort to return to Vancouver ended in tragedy when the plane crashed fifty feet from the summit of Mount Slesse, near Chilliwack, British Columbia.

Calvin Jones, a dominant football player despite a brief career, was killed. A number of other CFL stars were among the casualties.

Meanwhile, Grant returned to Winnipeg on the morning flight without incident. He called his wife, who had returned to Minnesota at the end of the season.

"Just after she finished talking to me, Pat got a call from her mother, asking if she had heard the news about me," said Bud. "She said she didn't know any news, but she'd just hung up from talking to me. Pat's mother had heard on WCCO Radio that a flight out of Vancouver was missing and presumed down, and that Bob McNamara and I were listed as passengers.

"The rescue teams were never able to get those people down off the mountain," said Grant. "They're still up there. It could have been all of us, so easily, not just Cal.

"I think about that."

6

Winnipeg

Why Grant?

He was only twenty-nine years old, and he had never coached.

However, there had been signs.

In his first year there, 1953, Bud was one of a group of players who prompted a change in the club's defensive tactics.

"George Trafton, our coach, believed in playing man-to-man defense," said Grant. "That way, it was easier for him to figure out who made the mistakes."

Grant and Neill Armstrong went to Trafton along with Dave Skrein and Billy Bye, both former Minnesota players, and requested that the club switch to a zone defense, better suited for the wider Canadian field and all the rollout passes.

"We were getting killed, trying to run with receivers in man coverage," Bud explained.

As a result of this meeting, Winnipeg went to the zone, where a player is responsible for a defined area, as opposed to specific receivers. That formation would become a Grant trademark. He wasn't aware at the time, but the Winnipeg club's executive committee heard about the four-player group.

There was another meeting.

During the 1956 season, Sherman's last at Winnipeg, the Canadian players made clear their disappointment with the treatment afforded them.

"It wasn't a team in turmoil," said Bud. "I don't mean to present it in that manner . . . but there were some things that needed to be talked out. I had always had a good relationship with the Canadians, so I spoke my piece . . . the usual thing, that we should stick together and not worry about anything except playing football, and if we did that, there would be the success that all of us were looking for."

Grant was called to Jim Russell's home for an evening meeting following his return from Vancouver. He found the Blue Bomber board of directors seated in the recreation room. There was a blackboard in the middle of the room. Russell ushered Bud in, handed him a piece of chalk, and said, "Show us how you'd beat Edmonton."

Grant laughed in the retelling of that adventure.

"I was relieved," he said. "I knew I could put anything up there, and it wouldn't be challenged. They were a fine group of fellows, but they didn't know much football."

Bud filled the board with Xs and Os and spoke in the football tongue. When the meeting was concluded, Russell said he would call him in the morning.

Grant spent that evening in two states: surprise and curiosity.

He had never entertained the notion of coaching. If truth be told, considering his career as a player, coaching would have seemed a least likely choice.

As a collegian, under Bierman in football and Cowles in basketball, Grant had railed against rules unless he could see the merit of them. That's fine, in theory, but something less in practice . . . the word "team" has to do with the group, not the individual.

As a professional, his talent level had been on a par with his balkiness at Philadelphia, when it came to accepting the wisdom of management.

The point being that Grant had been a ripple maker all along the way . . . emphatically, his own man. Management tends to view individualists with a narrowed eye.

That was the surface, of course.

Beneath it . . . and not even known to Grant, probably . . . was his equally consistent thread of fascination with and interest in coaches and the knowledge they had demonstrated.

Brown, Bierman, MacMillan, Cowles, Siebert, Kundla, Jim Trimble . . . he had absorbed bits and pieces from all of them. Some of it was how-not-to, to be sure, but knowledge nonetheless.

The curiosity dealt with money.

"I had no idea how much money coaches made. I just assumed they made a lot," said Grant. He was coming off a $11,500 salary as a 1956 player.

Russell called in the morning. He didn't offer the job, but he told Bud how much it would pay . . . $12,500.

Bud asked how long a contract would be involved.

"Contract?" Russell replied. "It would be for one year."

Grant returned to Minnesota and his family . . . Russell said they would get back to him.

The Grants discussed their situation.

There had been nothing to indicate that Bud would not play another four or five years.

"He was hurt badly that last year. It was the first time he'd had a serious injury," said Pat Grant. "But he had gotten over it, and I suppose we both assumed he would go on playing. Bud had talked some about having a fishing camp someday, but we didn't really have any plans."

Bud spent time reviewing the team he might take over.

"I thought we could improve the quality of the Americans, and I knew we had some good Canadians," he said. "We had a better team than the third place finish had indicated."

Would he be a part of it, a player-coach?

"They asked me that question at the first meeting," Bud answered. "I said I'd be one or the other, but not both."

Russell called on January 30, 1956. Bud was offered the Winnipeg coaching job and accepted.

That evening, the Grants entertained Wayne Robinson and his wife at dinner. A teammate both at Minnesota and Philadelphia, Robinson would join Bud as an assistant coach at Winnipeg.

At about three in the morning, the Grants were awakened by the telephone. It was Bud's brother Jim calling from California. Their father had died. On New Year's Eve, while announcement of his appointment was being made in Winnipeg, Bud was flying to California to attend his father's funeral.

Grant began a new chapter with his appointment as coach at Winnipeg, but in so doing ended another one.

His summers as a baseball player were over. Bud played his final baseball game for Hastings, Minnesota, in late July, just before leaving for Canada. He hit a home run in his last at bat, bringing Hastings from behind to win in an All-Star game.

"Of all the things we've done over the years," said Pat Grant, "I think the baseball games in the summer were the most fun."

When he arrived in Winnipeg, the local press asked Grant if he would become a resident or remain an import, as Sherman, his predecessor, had done.

"Allie was a very sound coach," said Bud, "but I don't think he ever really accepted Canada or that Canada accepted him. When the season ended, he went back to New York, and that didn't make him unique, because a lot of American coaches in Canada did that in those days. But it told the people where his priorities were . . . that he would be there only when he had to. The first thing I made clear was that I would live in Winnipeg."

The success Grant would build at Winnipeg had several factors at its base, among them good timing, good fortune, and good Canadians.

First on Grant's list of priorities was building up the Canadian players.

"If you tell a man he's good enough and if you tell him that often enough, eventually he'll begin to believe it himself. If you tell him the opposite or indicate it, he'll believe that, too."

The coaching philosophy that emerged in the summer of 1957 would remain with Grant down the years.

"It's important that players are treated equally, like your children. I don't care if they like me, but I want their respect."

He would earn that . . . and the Canadian-borns would play a key role in the earning. George Druxman, Ed Kotowich, Cornel Piper, Roger Savoie, Gord Rowland, Steve Patrick, Norm Rauhaus, Gerry James, and Lorne Benson were among the homegrowns that Grant would build upon.

And there were imports, too.

Ernie Pitts and Frank Gilliam came in as receivers in 1957 . . . Pitts went on to become the club's career reception leader, and Gilliam remains linked to Grant as scouting director for the Vikings.

Another expatriate from the Eagles arrived in Winnipeg in 1957, guard and linebacker John Michels. John played that year for Grant, spent the 1958 season as a college assistant coach at Texas A&M, and then rejoined Bud as an assistant coach in 1959. He's been with him ever since.

John Michels was not a big football player, though he had earned All-American honors at Tennessee. He was small and quick . . . and tougher than a ten-cent T-bone steak.

Without even the suggestion of a smile, Grant will recount a story involving Michels that he lists as one of his most astute coaching maneuvers . . . not to forget, however, that Grant can say some pretty outlandish things with a perfectly straight face.

"We were at Edmonton in the 1957 playoffs," said Bud. "The score was tied late in the game, and Edmonton had the ball, and they were on the march. They had a fine running back named Normie Kwong, and we hadn't stopped him all night. The game was to a point where, if Edmonton scored, it was going to be all over for us. I knew we had to do something, but I didn't have the foggiest notion of what the something should be. Kwong made another good run, and the situation was getting worse.

"I looked around and saw John Michels standing there. I said, 'Johnny, go in there and hit that little Chinaman as hard as you can . . . see if you can't make him fumble.'

"You know, that's exactly what happened. John Michels hit Kwong a ton, he came on a blitz, and I mean he just buried him. The ball flew out, and we recovered."

A smile danced across Grant's face.

"When people ask me if I remember any brilliant coaching moves that I made over the years, I tell the story of John Michels hitting Normie Kwong."

The 1958 import class also included a rangy quarterback from Iowa named Kenny Ploen. The name rhymes with "plain," but he wasn't.

Greg Fulton, CFL official and a long-time observer of the league, was asked to sort out Bud's success formula at Winnipeg.

"Good timing, for one thing," said Fulton. "Bud came in when Winnipeg had a group of good young Canadian players . . . they were ready to be improved upon. Bud recognized the importance of the Canadian players . . . he got the most out of them. I suppose that was his trademark, he got the most out of all his players. And, of course, he had Kenny Ploen. Kenny was the key."

Ploen had quarterbacked Iowa to victory in the Rose Bowl to cap a heroic college career. If you are old enough to remember *Jack Armstrong,* then you know about people like Kenny Ploen . . . the All-American boy.

There was one hang-up, however . . . Kenny Ploen wasn't sure he wanted to play professional football.

Ploen had been drafted in the NFL, but his college coach, Forest Evashevski, had discouraged Ploen from turning pro. An engineering student at Iowa, Ploen had a bright business future.

A tough case to crack, to be sure, but not too tough for Grant's indefatigable crony, Sid Hartman, the Minneapolis newspaperman.

Sid was, as the saying goes, "tight" with the Iowa coaches, particularly Evashevski and his bright young assistant, Jerry Burns. Indeed, Sid had made the introductions when Grant first met the Iowa coaches. Grant and Burns hit it off to a point where Burns spent several summers working in the Winnipeg training camp before fall practice began at Iowa.

Sid, through his friendship with the Iowa coaches, had access to Ploen. He caught up with him in northern Minnesota, where the Ploen family had a lodge. Sid based his pitch on Grant's being the sort of person Ploen would enjoy playing for.

It worked . . . which would come as no surprise, if you know Sid. If he's on a project, he moves with the relentless flow of the Mississippi River, only a good deal faster.

Sid stopped at Royalton, Minnesota, en route back to the Twin Cities. He called Grant from a phone booth.

"You've got your man," Sid announced.

Ploen would become the leader of the Winnipeg team.

A gifted athlete, but not at all flashy, he was precisely what he had been billed to be . . . a leader with intelligence and poise and, beneath an unruffled exterior, a fierce competitor.

Greg Fulton said of Ploen: "There were other quarterbacks who looked a bit fancier in their work, but what Kenny did was win. He knew how to win."

A few years later, Vikings General Manager Jim Finks was briefing an employee on his reasons for hiring Grant.

"He knows how to win," said Jim. "There are a lot of guys who know all the Xs and Os, but they don't all know how to win. Bud does, and more to the point, he knows how to live with winning."

Grant said of Ploen: "If you watched him in warm-ups before a game, his passes might not impress you. But let a receiver get open when the game was on the line, and he'd hit him.

"We won a Grey Cup when Kenny had a bad shoulder and couldn't play quarterback. Jim Van Pelt played there and had a fine game . . . he was selected the game's most valuable player, and he was most deserving. Kenny played halfback in that game, he blocked and caught passes and played safety on defense.

"He made an interception in the end zone that won the game for us. I don't mean to detract from what Jim Van Pelt did, but Kenny Ploen was the player who permitted us to win the game.

"He did what needed to be done."

Grant had been a teammate of the majority of his players just a year previous, and he was younger than many of them, but he experienced no difficulty in moving from within the ranks to head coach:

"I didn't feel a need to try and change myself. I was the same person . . . the only difference was I was the guy up at the blackboard instead of one of the people in the chairs. When I played, I believed in rules that made sense, but I didn't believe in rules just to have rules. That didn't change."

Winnipeg went 13–3 in Grant's first year and continued on to the Grey Cup.

The Western playoff matched the Bombers against Edmonton, and after two games the playoff series was even.

"We played the last game at Edmonton," said Bud. "If you counted everything, preseason games and all, it had to be the fifth or sixth time we had faced them that year. It was a night game, it was very cold, and the score was tied 2–2 at the end of regulation time."

And the CFL had no provision for overtime.

Jim Russell, the club president, went down to the field late in the game to see Grant.

"He wanted to know what to do if it ended up in a tie," said Grant. "There were two options . . . we could finish the game that night or come back the next day.

"Our team was beat-up physically. We'd come into the game with a lot of injuries, and it had been a tough game. I didn't know how good we could play in an overtime period, but I figured it had to be better than we would be the next day, so stiff and sore nobody could move. I told him we had to finish the game that night."

The two clubs went to their locker rooms after regulation time expired . . . CFL Commissioner Sydney Halter met with officials of the two teams.

"It was a big decision to be faced with," said Grant. Edmonton was the defending CFL champion. Winnipeg, the upstart that had captured the fancy of fans back home, had received thousands of telegrams before the game, wishing it well.

The decision came down after a twenty-minute wait: There would be overtime . . . not sudden death but a full quarter.

Down the years, one bit of bedrock Bud Grant coaching has had to do with "big plays."

"You go into a game knowing they'll be there," said Grant. "You don't know how many . . . maybe just a few, maybe more. And you don't know what form they will come in. But they'll be there, and they are the opportunities to turn a game around. The trick is to watch for them, to recognize them, and to respond to them."

Winnipeg took Edmonton off its throne with a big play that had all of the abrupt shock of a thunderclap.

Winnipeg kicked off to open the overtime period. The ball bounced into the end zone. Before the return man was able to emerge from the end zone, he was hit a smashing blow by Winnipeg's Roger Savoie . . . the ball bounded free, and Winnipeg recovered for a touchdown. The Edmonton crowd was shocked to silence.

"We got a single to go ahead 10–2, and we scored again when Ploen went about 40 yards on what was supposed to be a quarterback sneak," said Grant. "It just popped open. We won, 17–2."

When the team returned to Winnipeg the following day, their plane, propeller-driven, had to be stopped and shut down while still far out on the runway because of the wave of cheering Blue Bomber fans that swept onto the tarmac.

Winnipeg went to the 1957 Grey Cup against the Hamilton Tiger Cats, coached by Jim Trimble, who had coached Grant in his second season at Philadelphia.

"There was a lot of talk before the game," Grant recalled. "Trimble said they were going to beat us bad."

Trimble proved to be a man of his word . . . Hamilton crushed an outmanned Winnipeg team 32–7 in a game played in Toronto.

"They had a fine team, and we still had a lot of people hurt from the Edmonton game," said Grant. "It made for a poor combination."

It would be the last poor combination, from the Winnipeg point of view, when a Grant-coached team met a Trimble-coached team in the Grey Cup. The two teams met for the championship four times in the next five years, and the Blue Bombers won all four games.

But there was work to be done before that portion of the equation came to be fact.

And not all of it easy.

Winnipeg acquired another promising young player from Iowa for the 1958 season, tackle Frank Rigney, who would go on to be named to the CFL Hall of Fame. Rigney's arrival left Grant with a hard decision. Stav Canakes—a friend, a teammate, and, like Grant, a former Minnesotan—lost his spot on the Winnipeg roster to Rigney.

"Stav had been a good player, but it was obvious that Rigney had it over him," said Grant. "I had to tell Stav, who was a good friend, that he wasn't going to make it. He had a lot of trouble with that . . . he wanted to look for reasons other than the real reasons. We discussed it all of one day and part of the next. There was only one reason: I thought Rigney was a better player."

Did Grant have trouble moving on, once the decision was made?

"Making decisions is the biggest part of this business," he said. "A lot of people don't like to make decisions . . . oh, they like to gather information and express opinions, but they don't want to decide. Then, there are people who are so bothered by facing decisions that they make them just as fast as they can, just to get it over with.

"I take all the time I have available to decide something. Time is a tool, a part of the process, so I use all of it that's available to me. Things can change, things that might influence your decision."

And the decision, once made?

"Don't second-guess yourself," said Grant. "In this business, that's the key. If you can say to yourself, 'At that time, in the circumstances, it was the right thing to do,' then it was the right thing to do. You can't look back."

In 1958, Winnipeg launched a run of five consecutive first-place finishes in the CFL West and returned to the Grey Cup, against Hamilton, at Vancouver.

Grant calls it the most exciting football game he has ever been witness to. It was the game, referred to earlier, where Ploen squelched a last chance by Hamilton to preserve a 35–28 Winnipeg victory.

"It was a game of spectacular plays," said Grant. "Because we were the Western champion, the crowd was predominantly on our side. We blocked a punt in the end zone to finally get the lead . . . we had trailed 14–0 in the first quarter . . . and that stadium was bedlam."

Victorious Winnipeg fans had total recall when it came to Trimble's comment made before the game, when he said the Ti-Cats would "waffle" Winnipeg. "I can't imagine," said Grant, "how many waffles Trimble had sent to him by Winnipeg fans."

The 1962 Grey Cup was memorable but for other reasons.

"For years, the Canadians had wanted to showcase their game before a live American television audience," said Grant. "That 1962 game was the occasion." It marked Winnipeg's fourth Grey Cup victory in five years, but it is better remembered as the Fog Game.

"The fog rolled into Toronto's stadium as the game started and worsened as the day went on," said Bud. "On the field, we had no difficulty seeing what was going on, but the fog just hung there, like a blanket, over the field. Unfortunately, the television cameras, bringing the game live to the States, were at the top of the stadium. The television view was completely different from our view, down on the field. All you could see on television was the fog."

And that was a shame, Grant noted.

Right before the half, Winnipeg's brilliant running back, Leo Lewis, scored after taking a lateral from receiver Farrell Funston, who caught a pass, leaped high to avoid a tackle, and flipped the ball to Lewis.

"It was a super play," said Grant, "but the people watching the game on television didn't see it."

With nine minutes remaining and Winnipeg ahead 28–27, play was halted, and the decision made to conclude the game the next day. Winnipeg had the ball, facing second down and short yardage . . . the key down, since the Canadian game has only three downs instead of four.

"We had twenty-four hours to call that play," said Grant, "and we still didn't make first down."

But they did win . . . the nine-minute segment played on the following day proved uneventful.

"It had been an excellent game until they stopped play," said Grant, "but when we came back the next day, it just wasn't the same. The real tragedy, however, was that our great opportunity to show the game to Americans had been wasted."

Grant fielded winning teams in eight of his ten Canadian seasons. However he speaks with more intensity of his worst season than he does of his best.

In 1964, Winnipeg went 1–14–1.

"We won one, lost one, and tied one in our first three games," said Grant. "Then we lost thirteen games in a row. We lost nine starters to injury. Looking back, I doubt that we ever worked harder at coaching than we did that year. It was a good lesson, really . . . when you're winning, things aren't always going good as a result of what you're doing, and when you're losing, it doesn't necessarily mean that what you're doing is all bad. Things happen sometimes, and you can't explain them. The next year, we got the nine starters back and went to the Grey Cup."

Bud was head coach and general manager his last three years at Winnipeg, 1964–66.

"The one job can tend to inhibit the other," he said. "As coach, it's your job to convince a player that he's doing a good job. But when you sit down to negotiate a contract with him as general manager, you're coming from a different direction. It's difficult to take a fellow down a peg in negotiations, and then try to build him up out on the field."

With both jobs, Grant's off-season was a brief one . . . he'd pack a bag when the Canadian season ended and head for the United States in pursuit of college player talent.

"I carried a suitcase and a briefcase," he grinned. "The briefcase was full of blank contracts and a checkbook, and the suitcase was full of Hudson's Bay blankets and Crown Royal whiskey for people who did favors for us."

Bud has his war stories from the shadow world of football talent hunting.

He was in Charley Taylor's room at Arizona State in 1964, encouraging that great receiver to go to Winnipeg. Taylor had been a Number 1 draft pick by the Washington Redskins.

"Charley agreed to go," Bud recalled. "Then the phone rang. It was Chuck Drulis from the Redskins." Drulis asked Taylor how things were going. "Fine," said Charley, "I'm sitting here with a man from Winnipeg, and I'm going to sign to play in Canada."

Drulis talked Taylor into delaying the signing until morning.

"When I got to his place in the morning," said Grant, "Charley was gone."

Bud said he shook hands on an agreement with Alex Karras in the South Shore train station in Gary, Indiana.

"Alex said, 'Coach, I want to go up there with you,' " said Grant. There was good precedent . . . Ploen, Rigney, Gilliam, Bill Whisler, Sherwyn Thorson, and Ray Jauch all went on from Iowa to play at Winnipeg.

Indeed, Grant had recruited assistance from a former Gopher football teammate, Verne Gagne, to help Karras develop an off-season career as a pro wrestler.

But Karras signed with the Detroit Lions.

"They got to one of his brothers" was the way Bud explained it.

Grant rode herd on a Minnesota fullback named Roger Hagberg at the Senior Bowl . . . Hagberg was a draft choice of the Green Bay Packers.

"He was ready to sign, but he wouldn't do it until he'd talked to the Green Bay people," said Grant. "We sat there in a motel room, all night, calling the Green Bay guy every half hour. We finally got him, early in the morning."

In 1959, Jim Ausley was general manager of the Winnipeg team. Ausley reached an agreement with the New York Giants to acquire linebacker Jack Deleveaux on a one-year-loan basis. Deleveaux would play in Canada for the season, then be waived out of the CFL and return to the Giants.

Deleveaux went north and played for Winnipeg in 1959.

"The thing Jim neglected to do was make me aware of his understanding with the Giants," said Grant. "I didn't know Deleveaux was just there on loan." The Giants called Grant in the spring of 1960 to request initiation of procedures that would restore Deleveaux to their roster, according to their arrangement.

"What arrangement?" Grant asked.

When informed, he went to Ausley. "We were good friends, but I told Jim it was time to decide who he was working for, the Blue Bombers or the Giants. I called the Giants back and told them there was no deal, as far as I was concerned."

That done, Grant left promptly for Kentucky, where Deleveaux was on National Guard duty, to get the linebacker re-signed.

"I spent about twenty straight hours with him, convincing him to come back," said Bud. "I got it done and got out of there just ahead of the Giants."

Deleveaux returned to Winnipeg and played for six seasons. The Giants' Wellington Mara called Bud after the incident. "He told me I'd never get another player from the NFL, and I'd never get a job there," said Grant.

"I thought of that conversation a few years ago, when Well and I were visiting at a meeting," he said.

Did you mention it?

"No."

In 1961, Grant had been in Winnipeg four seasons as coach; his teams had played in three Grey Cups and won two of them. While the 1960 team didn't reach the final, it posted a 14–2 record and won the West.

In Minneapolis, Max Winter, who had owned the Lakers when Grant was a player, now was a partner in the fledgling Minnesota Viking franchise in the National Football League.

Max wanted Bud to be the Vikings coach.

"I know it's been said that I was offered the Viking job in 1961," said Grant. "I don't know that that is an accurate statement. Max told me I was his man and that he was lining up support . . . he asked me to think about it."

Grant did and decided his situation in Winnipeg, with an ascending team, was better than the uncertainties of an expansion franchise. He didn't think the timing was right.

"I told Max I didn't think I should be considered as a candidate," Bud said. "I've never known, to tell you the truth, if I was."

And he played out the Canadian string.

From the disastrous 1–14–1 record of 1964, the team battled back to finish 12–4 in 1965 and advanced to the Grey Cup for the sixth and final time in Grant's tenure. The Blue Bombers lost 22–16 to Hamilton in a game remembered as the Wind Cup, where punts frequently resulted in minus yardage as a result of near-gale winds.

In ten Canadian seasons, Grant's teams had won 105 games, lost 53, and tied 2. Factoring out the horrific 1–14–1 season of 1964, the record reads 104–39–1 for nine years.

Winnipeg finished 8–7–1 in 1966, Bud's last year. The record was good enough for a second-place finish in the West, but the irreversible business of change was in motion. Rowland and Savoie were gone, so was Leo Lewis. Ploen and Rigney were a year away from retirement. It had been a grand run, but there was retooling to be done.

There also was a new contract to be negotiated between Grant and the club.

It got done, but the results did not produce enthusiasm on Grant's part.

"I was prepared to spend the rest of my career in Winnipeg, going into negotiations," said Grant. "But I came out of them wondering if it wasn't time to move on."

Why?

Money differences. Also, a concern that the organization's philosophy on management of the club was changing.

"You can't put a pencil to everything," said Bud. "It doesn't always come out.

"You determine a budget, you work within it, and you try your best to stretch. But it's no different than your household budget . . . it doesn't always work. You have to recognize priorities, and sometimes you must make adjustments. In the past, I had done my job and kept the club advised of what I was doing. It worked fine . . . I think I did a good job of running the club, and I know I saved them money. If nothing else, I saved them money in my salary . . . I was one man, but I had two jobs.

"But during meetings after the 1966 season, I was told I would have to check out every decision with the board before it was made.

"I told them I didn't think that would work."

Negotiations were drawn out, and Grant became frustrated. "We weren't that far apart, maybe a couple thousand dollars. I didn't think I was asking to be overpaid. My feeling about money is, I'd rather work for you for a dollar too little than for a dollar too much . . . that way, I'm appreciated more. Finally, I said to heck with it and signed, but I wasn't comfortable. I felt like it might be time to move on."

The cause for moving on was in motion shortly, back in Minnesota.

Jim Finks had left his position as general manager of the Calgary CFL team in 1964 to take the same job with the Vikings.

The two men had been friendly rivals in Canada.

Grant savors the memory of a playoff game at Calgary during Finks's tenure . . . Winnipeg won on an astounding turn of fortune.

"We were trailing by one point with a minute or two remaining in the game," Grant recalled. "They had us backed up . . . it was third and 20, deep in our end. I remember our players looking at me as if to say, 'Well, coach, what's your third-and-20 play?' I didn't have one, but I also knew the only thing we could do was punt the ball and hope for something good to happen."

Something did.

Charlie Shepard punted the ball more than 70 yards, the kick rolling dead at the Calgary 10.

"We stopped them twice, forcing a punt," said Grant. "They had to kick out of their end zone, and the ball took a backward bounce so we ended up with great field position.

"We tried a field goal and missed, but the ball went into the Calgary end zone. They'd gotten a piece of the ball on the kick, because it was spinning wildly."

CFL rules provide several options for dealing with the ball kicked into your end zone, but the point is, you have to exercise one of them, or the kicking team is awarded a single or rouge point.

The ball may be run out of the end zone, punted out, or dribbled out, which means kicking the ball while it is on the ground.

Calgary, to Winnipeg's everlasting good fortune, elected a dribble kick.

"Because the ball was still spinning, their man didn't kick it squarely," said Bud. "The ball squirted forward, but it was still in the end zone. By kicking it, the Calgary player had left the ball 'live' . . . one of our players fell on it for a touchdown."

Jim Finks is nothing if not a practical man . . . and he put that disastrous dribble kick out of his mind when he went shopping for a new Vikings coach in 1967.

Norm Van Brocklin had led the club through its first five NFL seasons. The 1964 Vikings had risen above the frustration of three painful growth years to finish 8–5–1 . . . but, in 1965, they fell back to 7–7, and in 1966 skidded to a cheerless 4–9–1 mark as Van Brocklin and his bright young quarterback, Francis Tarkenton, forged philosophical differences that wouldn't be mended.

After that 1966 season, Tarkenton announced that he would be traded away from Minnesota . . . and Van Brocklin . . . or he would retire from football.

Finks obliged, sending Francis to the New York Giants for a clutch of high draft choices.

The pot continued to boil when Van Brocklin offered to resign. He had done so earlier, only to be persuaded to stay on. This time, his gesture was accepted.

With Van Brocklin's departure, there was no question in Finks's mind as to who the Vikings' new coach should be . . . his choice was Grant.

Bud isn't sure if Finks called him or he called Finks. "We had several occasions to talk to one another," Bud said. "Jim asked me if I would be interested in the job, and I said I would. He said, 'Fine, that's all I want to know right now . . . I'll get back to you.' "

At his end, Finks had been asked by Max Winter to interview several candidates, among them Nick Skorich and Bill Johnson.

"Why?" Finks asked. "Grant's the man for the job."

For window dressing was why, meaning the football business isn't much different than yours or the next guy's when it comes to politics and favors and so forth.

With the obligatory interviews behind him, Finks summoned Grant to the Twin Cities.

"We didn't discuss things in great depth," said Grant. "I had aways kept abreast of what was happening with the Vikings, so I had a fair idea of their situation. Actually, I'd been around there some. Several times, after our season, I'd go to the Vikings offices and look at film."

After an evening meeting, Grant was given time to sort out his thoughts.

"I suppose I didn't require much selling," said Bud. "If the negotiations at Winnipeg had gone differently, I might have. Jim came by my room later that evening and told me the job was mine if I wanted it."

Grant called his wife, Pat.

"She was elated, to say the least," said Bud.

Was she homesick for Minnesota?

"No, she liked Canada. But our kids were coming of an age where certain things were becoming more important. The Canadians had excellent secondary schools, but they offered less in the way of outside interests . . . music or drama, sports, things like that. She was looking forward to having all of those things available to our kids."

Bud was offered a three-year contract at $32,000, $34,000, and $36,000.

"I asked Jim if he could sweeten it any," said Bud.

"He said, 'Sure . . . thirty-four, thirty-six, thirty-eight.' "

Grant accepted and then returned to Winnipeg to advise the Blue Bombers that he was leaving. A week later he was announced as coach in Minnesota.

His summation on Canada and on a ten-year coaching experience of great success within that wide-open, exciting game with its fiercely proud fans?

"Times change, I know that. I can remember trips where the players would sing on the bus. I'm sure they don't do that anymore. The Canadian Football League was special to me in the time that I spent there.

"I think it was more important to the Canadians than the American game was to Americans."

7

Building a Viking Powerhouse

Bud Grant arrived in Minnesota in the late winter of 1967 and promptly defused suggestions that he would rebuild the Vikings.

"We want to grow," he said. "We want to build on what is already here. But we aren't rebuilding . . . the foundation of this team is already in place."

Odd . . . the Vikings, at least to the casual observer, seemed to have spent the first six years of their professional existence windsurfing from one emotional pole to the other, with far more time spent in the troughs than on the crests.

In the middle of the 1966 season, for example, when the Packers were at their zenith, the Vikings played like demons to win 20–17 at Green Bay, only to lose at home the next week to a mediocre Detroit team in a wave of pratfalls and blown assignments.

From 1961 through 1966, the Vikings were coached by Van Brocklin, a Hall of Fame quarterback with a house of mirrors personality.

Funny, combative, brilliant, brooding, gifted, mercurial . . . a lot of that last quality, mercurial. The toughest opponent the Dutchman ever faced was himself.

His team had rushed to early bloom in 1964, posting an 8–5–1 record and narrowly missing the playoffs. But they fell back after that. The 1966 team distinguished itself by leading the league in penalties en route to the 4–9–1 finish. The bottom fell out as Van Brocklin benched Tarkenton in December when the infant Atlanta team came to Minnesota. Tarkenton was from Atlanta, and the demotion mortified him. To complete the equation, Atlanta won the game.

Indeed, the casual observer might be forgiven for failing to notice that the foundation for progress was in place when Grant came back over the border in 1967.

But darned if he wasn't right.

79

Underneath all of the inconsistency and the hell-for-leather mind-set of Van Brocklin's term, there was talent on this football team.

Grant's Viking teams would win more than 150 games, and a lot of the winning would be done by people from those early years . . . Tingelhoff, Alderman, Sunde, Bowie, Cox, Brown, Osborn, Marshall, Eller, Larsen, Winston, Sharockman, and Kassulke.

And Grant got more help almost immediately.

Tarkenton was gone, traded to New York, but his price had been draft choices, and Jim Finks . . . operating from a hospital bed after gallbladder surgery . . . pumped new talent into the roster. Clint Jones and Gene Washington were first rounders from Michigan State . . . Bob Grim and Bobby Bryant came on the second round. Then Finks sent two veterans, Hal Bedsole and Tommy Mason, to the Los Angeles Rams for their first-round choice, and the move brought into focus the defense that would become the game's finest. The Vikings drafted Alan Page.

Bud Grant and Alan Page are not friendly, and Grant prefers to let matters rest at that. But their differences have done nothing to dilute Grant's respect for Page's awesome ability.

"He was the best defensive player I've ever seen," said Grant. "Alan was a great competitor . . . as much as he protested so many things about football, when the whistle blew, he couldn't overcome the fact that he was a great competitor.

"Very few people truly utilize their abilities," Grant went on. "Most people take their talents for granted . . . they come to depend upon them without ever thinking of trying to improve them. Alan worked at his ability, he made a great effort to improve himself. That effort made him a remarkable football player."

Actually, Grant knew a good deal about the Vikings . . . he read the Minnesota papers and talked to people and kept current over the years in Canada.

"I used to go to their office in the off-season and look at game films," he said. "The first few times I did it, Norm couldn't have been nicer . . . he told me to look at as much film as I wanted. Then, I went there one time when he saw me and said, 'What in the hell are you doing here? We can't have you hanging around here all the time!'

"That was the last time I went to their office."

One thing Grant knew that troubled him was the league-leading penalty total the club had drawn in 1966 . . . penalties aren't a ready mix with Grant's football philosophy.

Dave Osborn, the running back, recalled Grant's first year in Minnesota.

"Nothing upset Bud more than mental mistakes, and penalties are mental mistakes. He told us we couldn't afford to play dumb football, and penalties were dumb. He told us, too, that we would go from being the most-penalized team to being the least-penalized team . . . and we did. We still weren't good enough, but we quit doing dumb things," said Osborn.

The theory has been advanced that football teams are like families and that the head coach . . . ready or not . . . provides the father image for his players to mirror.

"The players were on Norm's wavelength when I got here," said Grant. "Looking at where they were and where I wanted them to be . . . there couldn't have been a much sharper contrast."

And where was it that Grant wanted them to be?

"Playing with discipline."

Which probably explains the bogus plea he made in 1967 training camp for a rule that didn't even exist.

At a team meeting, Grant told the players that the groundkeeper had asked their cooperation in avoiding an area of the field that had been newly sodded.

Of course, the groundkeeper hadn't said a word about the new sod.

"But I made a real point of it," Grant explained. "I sort of went overboard, explaining. I identified the area clearly, I said it was important for all of us to stay off it, and I said I didn't want anybody to forget about it."

Why did he do it?

"It's possible to make up a rule," Grant answered, "and learn about people by how they react to it.

"After I told the players about staying off the new sod, I went out on the field and watched.

"There were players who would come running up to the sodded area, recognize it, and go around it.

"There were players who would run onto it and then stop . . . you knew they'd forgotten and then remembered what I said after they started across. Those fellows would back up and go around.

"There were some who could come running out and go across the sodded area without even realizing it.

"Finally, there were fellows who just roared on across the sodded area, in defiance of what I had said."

And the moral of the story?

"It's important to learn things like that about people,"said Grant. "You learn who the players are who will forget what you tell them, you learn who will remember what you tell them, and you learn who just won't buy what you tell them. The same thing will happen in a game.

"That's why soldiers march in the army . . . nobody ever won a war by marching, you march to learn how to take orders as a group."

If it is possible for defensive linemen to have a good disposition, the Viking defensive tackle Gary Larsen fit that image. A big, sunny-faced blond, Lars was a nice guy.

But August two-a-days can try the patience of even the best disposition.

Gary Larsen gave in to one of those moments of tempest on the practice field at Mankato, and Grant, the new coach, was quick to seize his opportunity.

Larsen got into a fight.

"I don't even remember who the other player was," said Bud, "and the thing I knew, for sure, was that Larsen hadn't started it. But he fought . . . it was a brawl, and the two of them were flailing away at each other."

And then Grant flailed Larsen.

"It wasn't his fault that it started," said Bud, "but I needed to make a point. I really ripped into him, I had to . . . if it happened on the practice field it could happen in a game. Being undisciplined wasn't going to help us . . . you can't play football in a rage."

That first training camp had some sharp curves for the Viking veterans . . . they were Grant rules. As it had been in Canada, his list of player rules was short, but very sturdy.

"If you're going to have a rule, have a reason for it," he said.

Smoking, for instance.

Bud Grant detests smoking. One secret ambition he harbors to this day is to have his football team, en masse, come out publicly against the use of tobacco in any form.

His father died with a cigarette smoldering in his fingers . . . and as these pages were being written, Grant was serving as pallbearer at the funeral of his closest boyhood chum, a former smoker.

"I told them at that first camp that they could smoke if they insisted, but only in their rooms or in the john. They couldn't smoke in meetings or in the locker room or the dining hall or walking around the campus. I didn't make a big deal out of it . . . I just told them that was the way it would be. I knew they had smoked wherever they pleased when Norm was there . . . Norm was a smoker. Well, Norm wasn't there anymore, and I don't smoke."

He isn't keen on beer drinking in dorm rooms, either.

"I watched them lug those little refrigerators into the dorm when we moved in," he said. "I knew they had kept beer in their rooms in the past, although they were not supposed to, but I didn't say anything right away . . . I wanted to have a reason."

He had it several nights into camp.

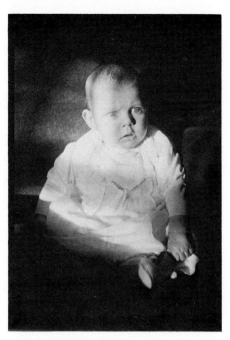

Bud at three-and-a-half months

Carrying the ball for the Superior Central H.S. Vikings

Bud (*top row, third from right*) played on a town basketball team in Superior.

Playing American Legion baseball in Superior

Speaking of Lettermen—

4 x 3 equals 12. That is, four years times three sports equals 12 letters. Although it is by no means a certainty, Harry (Bud) Grant is the current white hope to win 12 M's during his athletic career. If Grant, a freshman, accomplishes this feat, he will be the first Gopher 12-letterman in history.

Grant

Even before his football shoes had stopped swinging on a hook last fall, Bud had donned a basketball uniform. And before Dave MacMillan could say, "We need a good rebounder," Grant was first string forward.

In addition to his spectacular rebounding, 6 feet, 3 inch Grant racked up 25 points against Purdue last month to run his Big Nine total to 65 and his season total to 117. Although he isn't leading the Gophers in the scoring column, his average of .347 is high for the MacMillanmen.

Bud, a native of Superior, Wis., will make a bid for his third freshman letter when he reports for baseball practice this spring.

From the University of Minnesota daily

Posing for action with the Gopher varsity (*University of Minnesota*)

Bud and Pat at their wedding reception in the cabin at Forest Lake

Bud and Pat while he pitched summer baseball for Osceola, Wisconsin

Bud with his parents after returning home from the Navy in 1946

After a duck hunt, while he was at the University of Minnesota

While a student at the university, Bud was a model in a department store clothing ad.

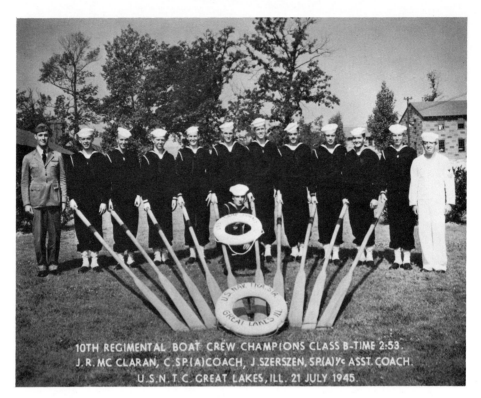

10TH REGIMENTAL BOAT CREW CHAMPIONS CLASS B-TIME 2:53.
J. R. MC CLARAN, C.SP.(A)COACH, J.SZERSZEN, SP.(A)Yc ASST. COACH.
U.S.N.T.C. GREAT LAKES, ILL. 21 JULY 1945.

Bud (*fifth from right*) with the Regimental Rowing Crew at Great Lakes

Bud makes a reception for the Philadelphia Eagles against the Cleveland Browns (in white uniforms) in 1952. (*Dick Olmstead*)

Driving to the basket for the Minneapolis Lakers, NBA Champions

A successful fishing trip while coaching at Winnipeg. *Left to right:* Bud, running back and punter Charlie Shepard, and assistant coach Wayne Robinson

Fly fishing near his summer home on Simms Lake (*John Croft*)

After the 1961 Grey Cup win over the Hamilton Tiger Cats, with Winnipeg mayor Steve Juba (*Bill Rose, Winnipeg Free Press Collection*)

Returning from the last Grey Cup win (*Hugh Allan, Winnipeg Tribune*)

Bud with two of his Winnipeg players, Gordy Rowland (*right*) and Charlie Shepard (*left*) (*Western Canada Pictorial Index*)

Bud with his Winnipeg staff: Joe Zaleski (*center*) and John Michels (*Winnipeg Free Press Collection*)

Bud on the sidelines with Winnipeg quarterback Kenny Ploen (no. 11) (*Gerry Cairns, Winnipeg Free Press Collection*)

On the sidelines at Winnipeg (*Winnipeg Football Club*)

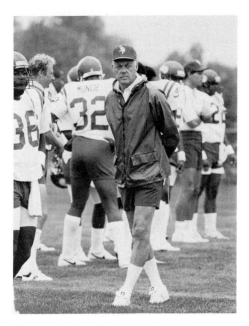

Bud with the late Senator Hubert H. Humphrey (*Minneapolis Tribune*)

The coach at work, Mankato training camp (*Rick Kolodziej*)

Bud with NFL Commissioner Pete Rozelle at Super Bowl VIII in Houston (*Lou Witt*)

Joe Kapp running the Viking offense in the snow at Metropolitan Stadium (*NFL Creative Services*)

Drew Pearson (no. 88) of Dallas after the "Hail Mary" reception in the 1975 NFL divisional play-offs. Nate Wright (43) of Minnesota is on the ground, and Paul Krause (22) is in the air. (*Dallas Cowboys Photos*)

Running back Ed Marinaro (no. 49) at Super Bowl VIII (*Malcolm Emmons*)

Alan Page (no. 88), Vikings defensive tackle, splits Green Bay blockers. (*Vernon J. Biever*)

Bud and Fran Tarkenton (*Vernon J. Biever*)

The Raiders pressure Fran Tarkenton (no. 10) during Super Bowl XI (*David Boss*)

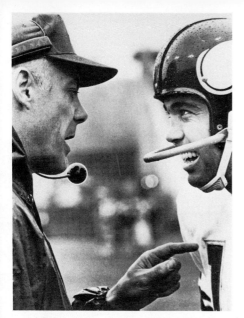

Bud holds a sideline conference with assistant coach Bus Mertes and quarterback Tommy Kramer (no. 9). (*Rick Kolodziej*)

Bud with Joe Kapp, Viking quarterback, on the day of Grant's first NFL victory, against Green Bay at Milwaukee (*Vernon J. Biever*)

Bud with forty-two-year-old place-kicker Jan Stenerud in training camp (*Rick Kolodziej*)

Dave Osborn (no. 41) blocks for Bill Brown (30). (*Vernon J. Biever*)

Linebacker Roy Winston (no. 60) (*Chance Brockway*)

Jim Marshall, defensive captain and end (no. 70 in white) (*Vernon J. Biever*)

Bud with Sid Hartman (*Rick Kolodziej*)

Mick Tingelhoff, Vikings' center (*Malcolm Emmons*)

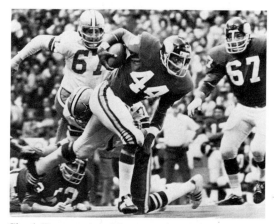

Chuck Foreman (no. 44) runs against Dallas in the 1973 NFC Championship Game. (*Vernon J. Biever*)

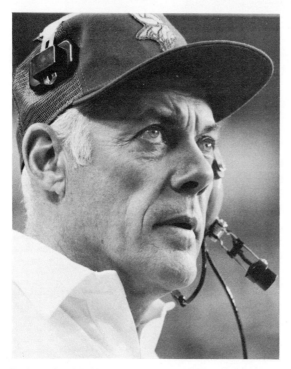

Bud on the sidelines during a game. (*Rick Kolodziej*)

Official recognition of his retirement—"Minnesota Celebrates Bud Grant Day" at the Metro Dome on September 2, 1984 (*Rick Kolodziej*)

Bud and Pat at home

Bud with his three sons: (*from left to right*) Bruce, Mike, and Danny

Christmas, 1984, with his grandchildren

During a team meeting, Grant prowled the player rooms in the dorm.

"Paul Flatley and Paul Dickson roomed together. I opened their fridge. There was a row of pop cans right across the front, but behind the pop, there was beer . . . they must have had a case of it. I mean, my kids could have done a better job of disguising it. I went back to the meeting and told them to have the refrigerators out of the rooms by the weekend."

If the veterans fretted that Van Brocklin had been replaced by a boy scout leader . . . and more than a few of them did, early on . . . their concern deepened when, before the first preseason game, Grant held National Anthem practice.

Athletes, in the main, seem to feel an obligation to fuss and fidget during the playing of the National Anthem.

They stand with hands on hips or twirling their headgear, and paw the grass or roll tight neck muscles, all the while chewing mightily at a wad of gum. If you haven't see a hockey goalie whanging his pads into place over the "rockets red glare," then you've probably noticed a linebacker repositioning his athletic supporter and its contents with "bombs bursting in air."

The one thing very few of them do is stand still.

Grant did away with "antsy anthems" in short order.

"I suppose this sounds corny today," he said, "but I believe in the National Anthem. I feel good about it. I know that attitude is passé for many people, but my feeling for my country has a high priority. I grew up during a war, and I spent my youth preparing to go to war. About the only thing left today out of all that is respect for the flag . . . it's really our last demonstration of patriotism.

"There are a lot of times when I still get misty-eyed at the playing of the National Anthem."

If not misty-eyed, Grant's charges would at least hear the playing of the anthem in an orderly fashion.

Several days before the first 1967 preseason game, Bud looked over his squad for someone who was big and had had military training of some sort.

He settled promptly on Carl Eller, a vast defensive end called Moose. Eller had been in the National Guard. He also enlisted John Kirby, a linebacker and another Guardsman.

"I said, 'Moose, if you stand up there tall during the playing of the anthem, people are going to respect you for it.'

"He bought it," said Grant. "We went over how the players should stand . . . every man on a yard line, heels together, eyes front, left arm at your side, helmet in your right hand. Then I asked Eller to take the rookies aside and teach them. He not only did it, he was enthusiastic about it, he was proud to be chosen as the model. When you want to set a new thing into motion, you have to pick the right people to lead for you."

Carl Eller played defensive end for the Minnesota Vikings for fifteen years . . . expertly, but the end of his playing career was bittersweet. Eller retired from football with drug and alcohol problems.

But he didn't stay that way.

Through treatment, through the support of others, and through his own belief and courage, Moose is recovering today. More than that, he has visited NFL teams across the country, working in the effort to educate athletes to the truth of alcohol and drug use.

"One of my biggest regrets," said Eller, "is that I didn't get closer to Bud as a player. I really learned from him after my playing days were finished. I wish now that I could have modeled myself after him."

The Vikings practiced standing at attention for the National Anthem . . . they even practiced singing.

They went to Tulsa, Oklahoma, that weekend to play the Philadelphia Eagles . . . the irony was not wasted on Grant . . . and won, 34–0. And their anthem formation was letter-perfect.

"People can only keep their eyes on the flag for so long during the playing of the anthem," Grant explained. "After that, they look at other things. What is the most logical thing to look at at a football game? The players. And not just the fans . . . the players on opposite sides of the field are looking at each other.

"It's a form of discipline . . . if the player across the field sees you chewing gum or scratching your butt, that's one thing. But if he sees you standing tall, taking pride in the way you look, he'll notice. He might not want to, but he's going to respect you for it."

Admirable as the new-wave discipline might be, the Vikings had hired Grant for more simplistic reasons. . . .

To win, for instance.

Shortly before Grant went to Minnesota, Jim Finks, the man who had hired him, talked about Bud.

"There will be things about him that you don't understand," said Finks. "He won't always communicate why he does something the way he does, and even when he does, it might not make sense to you.

"But he knows how to win, and, more important, he knows how to live with winning."

Grant was asked what Finks's words meant to him.

"It's harder to live with winning than it is to live with losing," he said.

"Green Bay did a good job of it, back when they were having their run. Lombardi got a lot of credit, and I'm sure he played an important role in their success, but I think a lot of it had to do with being in Green Bay. Achieving and holding on to success is more attainable in a small city like Green Bay than it is in a big city. There just are fewer distractions in Green Bay than there are in Los Angeles or New York.

"The difficulty comes in remembering what it took to get you there, to be successful in the first place," said Grant.

"When you're winning, everybody wants a piece of you. Suddenly, there are opportunities for distraction, the notoriety that goes with winning. We all want to be recognized for our accomplishments, but that recognition, unless you guard against it, can carry you further and further away from the attitude that permitted you to become a winner.

"Players can become so involved in the things surrounding the game . . . the distractions . . . that they have to fight to be on time for practice, instead of hanging around the locker room, waiting for practice to start. I guess you can call that coping," said Grant, "the need to be able to deal with success and the price you must pay for it."

Minnesota . . . relatively isolated in the geographic sense and solid in its Scandinavian heritage . . . struck Grant as a promising site for long-term success.

Fair enough . . . Grant knew how to live with winning, but the Vikings still needed to learn how to win.

And to Bud's eye, they needed a quarterback with which to do it.

At the midpoint of 1967 training camp, Grant met with Finks late one evening in his dormitory apartment.

The Viking quarterbacks at that point were Bob Berry, John Hankinson, and Ron VanderKelen . . . good men, all, but not of the level Grant was seeking. The level Grant was seeking, Tarkenton, had been dealt to the Giants.

"Got a ways to go at quarterback, eh?" Finks opened.

Grant cocked an eyebrow, sitting on a straight-backed kitchen chair.

"Well," said Finks, "I think we can get him . . . it'll take some doing, but I think we can."

Grant chewed his lip.

"Then you'd better get him," he replied.

"You know him," Finks countered, "you know what you'll be getting."

Grant shrugged. "I know . . . I also know he's better than anything we've got."

A bysitter asked whom they were talking about.

"Joe Kapp," Finks answered. "A quarterback up in Canada named Joe Kapp."

The fellow said he'd never heard of him.

Finks laughed briefly. "You will," he replied.

Joe Kapp.

"Forty for sixty . . . hell, it could be thirty for sixty or a hundred for sixty. All it means is every guy on the team giving it everything he's got for sixty minutes."

If the Pied Piper of Hamelin had played football, he would have worn jersey Number 11.

"It's real nice that you should select me for this award, but I can't take it. There ain't no Santa Claus, there ain't no Easter bunny, and there ain't no Most Valuable Viking."

Joe Kapp went from the University of California at Berkeley to Calgary of the Canadian Football League. He was first signed as a pro by Finks. He went from Calgary to Vancouver, and before he joined the Vikings, there was a dalliance with Houston of the old American Football League.

Envision, if you will, Anthony Quinn in his Zorba role . . . but dressed as a football player and with less nose. That was Joe.

Roistering, swashbuckling, fearless.

Once, after a tough loss, Joe and Lonnie Warwick, the Vikings middle linebacker, attended a players-only gathering at somebody's house. Kapp and Warwick stood in the kitchen, glumly nursing their beers.

"I lost the damned game," Joe growled.

Lonnie glared at him. "The defense lost the game," he declared. Most people would have been happy to let the discussion end right there . . . Lonnie Warwick was rougher than the back end of a bowling alley.

Kapp finished his beer and responded in that gravel tone of his . . . when you're talking tough, Joe would get mentioned before you ran out of breath.

"You're full of crap," he suggested.

Then they went out into the backyard and fought for fifteen minutes or so. Kapp showed up for practice the next day with dark glasses to match twin shiners . . . Warwick's nose had several new angles to it.

Truth be told, Kapp was Van Brocklin's kind of guy . . . what was a straight arrow like Grant doing with him?

Trying to win.

And Joe Kapp . . . with a gait remindful of Dagwood Bumstead running for the bus and throwing passes that frequently resembled gut-shot mallards . . . knew how to win.

"He became the image of the Vikings, really," said Grant. "The thing about Joe, he was a competitor. He'd battle anybody. That quality, his toughness, drew players to him. A lot of quarterbacks seem special, kind of set apart from the rest of the team. But not Joe . . . Joe was one of the troops."

How did Grant and Kapp get along?

"Fine," said Bud. "I liked Joe . . . everybody liked Joe, he's a likable guy. In this business, you play the people who get the job done, and Joe did that."

Uniquely.

He was a big man for the position, and he ran with a shambling, rusty-kneed stride . . . through or over people, never around them. His passes, judged on appearance, were never mistaken for those of Unitas or Namath. Fine . . . when the end zone was in sight, Joe Kapp would figure out a way to get a Viking into it. He had the dark, soulful eyes of his Mexican heritage, a rasping burr of a voice that always seemed to be just an inch off laughter, and a strong jaw, made more noticeable by a jagged scar, the souvenir of a broken bottle in a Canadian misadventure.

The Vikings went to the playoffs for the first time after the 1968 season . . . and became a 24–14 victim of the Colts at Baltimore. The Vikings had youth and enthusiasm . . . the Colts had Unitas and a defense like a loan shark's muscle on the Jersey docks. Kapp passed for a lot of yardage, but he took a frightful pounding, hammered down, time after time, into the chill, mustard-colored mud of Memorial Stadium.

The next year, the Vikings opened their home season against those same Colts and beat them 52–14 . . . and Joe Kapp threw seven touchdown passes to match the NFL single-game record.

Afterward, in a jubilant locker room, Kapp thrust a grimy fist high in the air and roared, "Remember the Alamo!"

The 1967 Vikings lost their first four regular season games . . . Grant's first NFL coaching victory came in his native Wisconsin, at Milwaukee, against the defending NFL champion Green Bay Packers.

Kapp set a Viking record that day . . . fewest pass completions in one game. He completed two.

It was a rainy day, and Grant's game plan was very basic . . . keep up pressure on defense and try to avoid mistakes on offense.

Kapp chafed under Bud's conservative game plan.

"Whenever there was a time-out, Joe would come to the bench scowling, and say, 'When are we gonna open up?' I told him we weren't going to open up. That was a great football team we were playing, we couldn't afford to take chances and risk turning the ball over. I told Joe to be patient . . . I said we'd get an opportunity if we kept on sawing wood."

The opportunity came in the fourth quarter.

With the score tied 7–7, the Vikings sent fullback Bill Brown hurtling into the Green Bay middle on five consecutive plays.

"We'd been running Brown up the gut all game," said Grant. "He was gaining yards . . . there was no reason to go away from it."

Grudgingly, Green Bay packed its defense inside to stop Brown's furious charge.

When that happened, Grant sent in a play and a message . . . and answered his quarterback's plea.

"Open them up."

Kapp faked beautifully to Brown on play-action and then registered his second pass completion of the day, a 30-yarder to set up the game-winning field goal by Fred Cox.

"Joe told me after the game," said Grant, "that he never would have believed he could feel like a contributor on a day when he completed just two passes. But he did . . . he was happier than anybody."

Joe Kapp left Minnesota after the 1969 season . . . and Bud Grant said that wasn't surprising, either.

"It was his history. When Joe went to Calgary, they had some success, and he took them there. Then he pulled out his pistol.

"He went to Vancouver, and it happened pretty much the same way. He came to Minnesota, we made it to the Super Bowl, and Joe pulled out his pistol. Finally, he tried to pull it on the game itself." Grant referred to contract disputes that marked Kapp's career. After Minnesota, he played briefly for the Boston Patriots. His final assault was, as Bud said, against the system . . . an unsuccessful lawsuit challenging the validity of the NFL player contract.

Like Grant said, though, everybody liked Joe Kapp.

A national writer was interviewing Joe once, out on the lawn, while Kapp watched his son, J.J., frolic on playground equipment.

The interview was concluded, and Joe stood to leave for practice. J.J. shouted at him.

"Come swing me, Dad!"

Kapp grinned that great grin of his and shook his head.

"Can't, son . . . I gotta go swing Mr. Grant's offense."

And swing it he did.

If acrimony may be put on the back burner . . . which isn't a bad place for it . . . and if you like to watch football played with great passion, then Kapp was your man. In a time when the struggling young Vikings needed a genuinely tough guy to break trail, Joe Kapp was a marvelous choice.

The 1967 Vikings, Grant's first team, finished 3–8–3, but four of the eight losses were by six points or less.

Finks, the canny scrounger of player talent, saw to it that Grant's 1968 team was better-fixed.

The draft brought Ron Yary, a behemoth who would play offensive tackle for fifteen years. It brought Charlie West, too, a gifted defensive back, and Oscar Reed, a running back. Then Finks traded for Gary Cuozzo, a scholarly quarterback, and grabbed receiver John Henderson off the waiver wire. Then, with low draft-choice swaps, he acquired linebacker Wally Hilgenberg from Pittsburgh and free safety Paul Krause from Washington. Both arrived wearing the "damaged goods" label that presages so many player trades . . . they were available because somebody else didn't want them. Hilgenberg was judged too wild to tame, Krause was said to be too timid.

Wally Hilgenberg played twelve years for the Vikings, fitting into Grant's discipline-laden system, and Krause played the same, ending up as the most productive pass interceptor in NFL history.

Further on, the Vikings acquired receiver Ahmad Rashad from Seattle on similar grounds . . . the Seahawks weren't happy with him.

"The point in all of this," said Bud, "is that these were good people, but for some reason, they weren't appreciated where they were. Sometimes, a club isn't comfortable with excellent players, maybe they feel threatened by them.

"When you get a player with true talent, you don't coach him very much. You show him your system, but it's like baseball . . . if you've got a guy who's hitting .370, stay away from the batting cage, don't try to improve his stroke! Don't mess with him. But a lot of coaches can't do that. They'll take a true talent and try to coach him. I don't know if it's because they want credit for his ability . . . I just know that if a man's got the talent needed, stay away from him. You encourage him, you give him what help he needs, but you don't try to change him. That's like saying we deserved credit for coaching Chuck Foreman . . . forget it. Give him the ball . . . that was all the coaching he needed."

Safetyman Krause spoke of Grant's impact upon him.

"I learned quite a bit from Bud," he said, "but the most important thing he taught me was to be myself. Do the things you do best and do them to the best of your ability . . . but know your limits, and don't try to do what you can't do.

"Bud, truly, was a player's coach," said Krause. "He never asked you to do the impossible. A lot of coaches can put the Xs and Os on the blackboard, but if it doesn't come off in the game the way they had it drawn on the board, they get frustrated. Because he had been a player, Bud knew what an athlete could do. He handled players so darned well . . . I suppose he handled us the way he would have liked to have been handled as a player."

Although Baltimore abbreviated it, Minnesota's "glory run" had its origins in the 1968 season.

The Vikings finished 8–6 to win the National Football Conference Central Division for the first time. They yo-yoed through the first twelve games, standing 6–6 at that point, although they had defeated Green Bay twice, the first time a Minnesota team had managed to do that.

The last two regular season games were on the road . . . at San Francisco and Philadelphia. The rain-sodden turf in Kezar Stadium was perfect footing for the combative Kapp . . . he slogged through shoe-top-deep goo for a vital touchdown as the Vikings won 30–20. In the finale, at Philadelphia, Minnesota won 24–17 in the snow, with Brown and Osborn battering the Eagle defense.

But even with two closing victories, the Vikings needed help. Green Bay played at Chicago on that final Sunday of the season, and unless the Packers won, Chicago would beat the Vikings out of a playoff berth at Baltimore.

After the Philadelphia game, Grant and a few others sat in the locker room at Franklin Field, listening as Sid Hartman, the sports columnist, talked long-distance to Chicago and relayed a play-by-play of sorts of the Bears–Packers game at Wrigley Field.

Green Bay nursed a slender lead late in the game, but Chicago was on the march.

What Sid may have lacked in style, he more than made up for in fervor.

"No gain! Packers stopped them for no gain."

And we'd holler and speak of our admiration for the Packers, which was a crock, except that circumstance can lead to strange bedfellows.

Then Sid's face would fall. "First down . . . the Bears made first down." And we would groan.

All of us, that is, except Grant.

He sat on the corner of a rubbing table, flipping a roll of tape. All of his concentration looked to be given over to flipping that tape.

Things in Chicago were getting desperate . . . the Bears were a play or two away from field-goal range, and a field goal would win it. I watched Grant and marked on how perfectly he flipped that tape . . . each toss achieved exactly the same height.

Sid's voice soared as a big play unfolded.

"Pass . . . they're gonna . . ."

And then he shrieked.

"Nitschke . . . Nitschke! Interception! Nitschke intercepted, and Green Bay's got the ball! It's all over!"

There was not even a flutter of change in Grant's expression, but that final tape flip hit the locker room ceiling.

Minnesota was apologized into the playoffs by the national press . . . the Vikings were newcomers to the tournament, and Baltimore, with Unitas, had regal status.

Grant didn't accept that sort of logic.

"Getting into the playoffs is what counts," he said. "Once you do that, anything can happen. I don't accept people saying, 'This team belongs in the playoffs,' or 'This team doesn't.' If you get there, you belong."

But, still . . . how does a coach approach a game he knows his team isn't likely to win?

In Canada, when Grant's Winnipeg team won in the Grey Cup for the first time, it trailed Hamilton 14–0 before the first quarter was over. After the game, a Winnipeg player was asked how the players had reacted to falling behind quickly to a team that had whipped them soundly in their first championship meeting.

The player said he and his mates had watched Grant for their clue.

"We looked at the coach," he said. "He didn't seem upset, so we figured we didn't have any reason to be upset."

"That stuck with me," said Grant. "If my remaining calm could influence players, then it had value."

Grant approached the 1968 playoff at Baltimore with that dread calm the NFL would come to recognize in years to come.

"Players take their cue from the coaches," he said. "If the coaches don't have enthusiasm or are not optimistic, the players will pick up on that attitude. You have to be realistic, but you can't get down. Our job is selling a system to the players, and they are both curious and intelligent. Ultimately, they want to have faith in what they're doing. We have coaches' meetings where someone will really unburden himself on how a certain player just isn't good enough.

"That's fine . . . that's where things like that should be said. But once you leave that coaches' meeting room, you never, never say anything against your own players.

"You can have a man, and you know he's not good enough . . . but until you have somebody who is better, you keep your mouth shut, and you do everything you can to help that man."

A lot of football coaches . . . like the rest of us . . . tend to what-if.

If you're a football coach, what-iffing can surface in the evaluation of players.

There is a temptation, in preparing for a game, to tell yourself, "Now, if our Charley can really make a super effort and play his very best against their Roscoe, we're going to be fine." And once in a while, that happens . . . it happens about as often as you get raises or your wife goes all day without speaking. More often, "our Charley" gets every last what-if knocked out of him by "their Roscoe," because Roscoe's better than Charley. And, oddly, statements of this sort continue to be made, even though the coach knows . . . both in his heart and in his film cans . . . that it isn't true.

Why?

Because we prefer to think happy thoughts, is why . . . they're more pleasant.

Bud Grant what-ifs about as often as you vacation on the Black Sea.

Privately, Grant looks at Charley-versus-Roscoe and says, "We're going to lose that one . . . let's look for a way to offset the loss."

Publicly, of course, he does nothing of the sort, because the Charleys of our business still have to go out there and line up against the Roscoes.

"The player will respond to your approach," said Grant. "If you let him know you're convinced he can't handle a man, he's beat before he starts. So you don't make a big deal out of it, you treat it matter-of-factly. If your man is going up against Merlin Olsen, and you know Olsen's the best there is, you still say, 'All right, now here's the way we're going to block Olsen.'

"You can't delude yourself," Grant explained. "A lot of coaches do that, and they get stung. There are coaches who can't win with superior talent, but there aren't any coaches who are going to win consistently with inferior talent. And you can't fall into the trap of deluding yourself to think that your coaching is going to turn an inferior player into a superior player. But a lot of coaches do that."

The Vikings opened the 1969 season against the New York Giants at Yankee Stadium. The Giants won, 24–23, on a zany play authored by their new quarterback, Tarkenton. He threw a lob pass for tight end Bob Tucker, who was sandwiched between two Viking defenders. Paul Krause swiped at the ball, barely touching it. It dribbled down Bobby Bryant's back. By that time, Tucker was flat on his back. The ball dropped into his hands for a completion.

It would be Minnesota's last loss for quite a spell. Beginning the following Sunday with Kapp's fiesta against Baltimore, the Vikings reeled off twelve straight wins before losing 10–3 at Atlanta on a day better suited for mud wrestling than for football. Falcon defender Claude Humphrey picked up a fumble and sloshed fifty yards through a downpour for the game's only touchdown.

Over the span of twelve wins, the Viking defense gave up just 99 points. For the fourteen-game season, the defense allowed 133 points, a league record for the modern era. Going four for November against the Bears, Browns, Packers, and Steelers, Minnesota scored 143 points and allowed 41. The biggest game of that run came at Los

Angeles against the Rams . . . Minnesota had won ten straight, the Rams had won eleven.

The Vikings won, 20–13, sparked by Charlie West's long return of the opening kickoff.

Charlie was good at that . . . Charlie was part Apache and all athlete. In 1968, Charlie ran a punt back 98 yards to score against the Redskins. When he got to the bench, Grant cocked an eyebrow.

"If you ever field a punt at the 2-yard line again," he said, "you're out of here." The rule of thumb for return men is, Don't touch anything inside your 10.

One memorable sidebar to that big win at Los Angeles was made possible by John Michels, the fiery Vikings offensive line coach.

Michels spent the week leading up to that game jawing on Yary, the big rookie tackle from Southern Cal.

"You wanta go out there, play in the Coliseum in front of all the fans who know you, and get embarrassed?" Michels would holler. "You're going up against Deacon Jones, for God's sake . . . unless you get going, he'll destroy you!"

On the first play after West's kickoff return, Yary blocked poor Deacon about twenty-five feet straight back . . . he ran him right into the end zone. As the day wore on, it was Yary who destroyed the Deacon.

Afterward Michels had a word for his big rookie.

"You played pretty good," he said. "Of course, you have to remember, Deacon's not as young as he used to be."

Michels has been with Grant for nearly thirty years.

"The Canadian years were special," he said. "When we were there, there was still sort of a pioneering flavor to football . . . they weren't as advanced, in many ways, as it was in the States. I can remember the dressing rooms with one shower and an old potbellied stove . . . I feel fortunate that I was able to participate in that time, because it's gone, now."

Why has Grant succeeded, in John's estimation?

"I think of two reasons . . . one will sound like I'm blowing my own horn, but I'm not. That is his ability to choose assistants. He's very selective, and there have been a couple of exceptions, but once you get the job, you know it's yours so long as you perform. Bud gives his assistants freedom and responsibility, he allows you to do your job.

"I think the other element is his great flexibility in dealing with players . . . he's a wonderful student of human nature."

The assistant coaches prepare the weekly game plans during the season, Jerry Burns coordinating the offensive plan and Bob Hollway the defense. Bud receives a copy of the finished product.

"He certainly has veto power over it, but I don't ever recall him telling us to change something," said Michels. "He might ask a question, but he really doesn't get involved with the strategy, the nuts and bolts of preparing for a game.

"Not to say that we haven't disagreed . . . we've had some hellacious, knock-down-drag-outs over the years. I'm not one to be a yes-man, and eventually it has to come to his saying, 'We'll do it my way because I'm in charge.' That's fine, I can appreciate that. The thing about Bud, though, he picks his spots . . . he's very deliberate. If he decides to run with something, he's thought it out very carefully in advance . . . he doesn't like surprises."

You get a thread running through conversations with Grant's people . . . they might say it in different ways, but they all end up the same place.

Bud Grant doesn't really coach football in the sense his title usually implies.

He oversees it.

"The assistants would do 98 percent of the coaching," said Carl Eller, "but the 2 percent Bud did seemed like it made the difference.

"You need a coach for direction and for his ability to remain outside the emotion of the game. Bud could do that . . . he was always a couple of steps removed from the moment. I think the need he filled was being someone to oversee the whole game and not worry about being involved in every play."

"He's demanding on the field," said Mick Tingelhoff, "but he turns the responsibility for self over to you. He wants you to coach yourself, really."

Tarkenton: "He doesn't clutter his mind with a lot of play-calling mechanics. That leaves him free to manage the game. He's the best on-field coach I've ever seen."

"He didn't coach a lot, as you tend to think of coaching," said Dave Osborn. "I think part of that was because he surrounded himself with good people. Part of it is his approach, too . . . Bud's more like the chairman of the board out there than a coach. But he was never far from you, never distant. I can remember practicing on Saturdays before big games . . . really big games . . . and I'd be getting pretty wound up. You wouldn't see him come up, but all the sudden he'd be there. It might be an elbow in the ribs, and he'd say, 'Did you see those geese fly over?' "

Paul Krause spoke of the side of Grant the fans will never see.

"He fooled a lot of people. People outside just saw that gray hair and the steely eyes. He wasn't that way with us, he was close to his football family. I think the fans, around here at least, see Bud in a way that is almost larger than life . . . they have him up on a pedestal. The great thing of being a player was knowing that wasn't true . . . he was right down there with you, competing."

The Vikings went 12–2 during the 1969 regular season.

There is a point in the development of a football team that is very special, a true, pure point. It is when a good team becomes great.

The Vikings reached that point on December 27, 1969, in snow-rimmed Metropolitan Stadium when they hosted the Rams in the first playoff game.

If the Rams had been beaten on their home field by Minnesota earlier, they were determined to return the favor in the playoff.

And very nearly did.

In the final analysis, they had no answer for the fierce defensive rush of Marshall, Eller, Page, and Larsen, and for the fury of Joe Kapp.

Kapp drove the Vikings to victory. He jammed his wobbly passes through coverage and goaded and cussed his running backs for more yardage. His approach was as elementary as a mule skinner taking the whip to his team.

Appropriately, the decisive touchdown was left to Kapp . . . operating in close to the Ram goal line, he rolled to his left with the option to pass and then galloped toward the corner of the end zone. He hurdled a diving Los Angeles linebacker at the chalk, tumbling headfirst into the end zone and national prominence.

After that game, Joe Kapp was philosophical.

"Everybody wants to win," he growled. "Hell, wanting to win is nothing! Show me the people who are willing to do what it takes to win . . . you gotta be willing, not wanting!"

The Vikings eliminated the Rams 23–20 . . . a week later, in the NFL championship game, they thrashed the Cleveland Browns 27–7 in the chill of the Met to qualify for the Super Bowl.

Kapp opened the Cleveland game with a bomb to Gene Washington and then removed all doubt of the outcome with an impromptu scoring dash of his own.

The play was designed as a handoff to Bill Brown, only Brown ran the wrong hole. As Kapp spun to hand off, Brown crashed into him. Both men reeled, but Kapp recovered, wheeled back toward the goal line, and scored over Browns linebacker Jim Houston. He hit Houston so hard that the Cleveland stalwart was forced from the field with a concussion.

In retrospect, the Vikings' win over Los Angeles in the first round of the 1969 playoffs looms as the most significant in the history of the franchise.

That emergence had been built upon by Grant . . . carefully, patiently, and with attention to every detail, no matter how niggling.

Complacency is an ill the coach guarded against . . . sometimes in small ways and at every level.

When the Vikings went to Mankato State for their second training camp under Grant, the college staff was receiving high marks and a fair amount of publicity for its efforts to quarter the team in good style. Not escaping Grant's scrutiny was the fact that the college enjoyed the attention.

"They were taking bows," Bud pointed out. "That can be dangerous. If they can take themselves too seriously, they can take us for granted."

Going into that second camp, Bud knew the college hadn't done all the preparatory work on the practice fields that the Vikings had requested. That troubled him.

But not for long.

When Grant met the press at the end of the first day of practice, his opening line went something like this:

"The condition of the practice fields is a disgrace."

The college, of course, was appalled . . . but beginning that very evening, the condition of the fields improved by leaps and bounds.

In another training camp, the director of the college food service was featured in several articles praising his work, and the food was good, no argument there. And the fellow was pleased by the publicity.

But Grant began to watch.

A few days later, moving through the chow line at lunch, he picked deliberately through a basket filled with cello-wrapped packages of soda crackers.

He picked, until he found the package he wanted . . . one that had an open, frayed edge. Grant walked back to the food service manager, who was standing at the head of the line, joshing with players.

Bud flipped the offending packet to the man and impaled him upon that ice-blue stare.

"You're supposed to feed us," he said, "not mice."

The war against complacency was not limited to noncombatants.

"You can get after a player," Grant conceded, "but only a star."

Receiver Sammy White, the most proficient pass catcher in the club's history, was a target.

It was just another day on the practice field and just another pass. And Sammy dropped it.

Grant walked across the field to intercept White as he trotted back to the huddle.

"I don't ever want to see you do that again," he advised. "To see another fellow drop a pass is one thing, but you have a great talent, you have been blessed with an ability that very few people have. I don't ever, ever want to see you drop a ball like that."

Grant turned and walked away, leaving Sammy to ponder the burdens of stardom.

"Obviously," Grant explained, "it's impossible to go through practice and games, day after day, and never drop a pass. But by demanding it and making a point out of it, it made an impression. I don't have the figures to back it up, but I think Sammy's concentration improved after that."

On Grant's acceptance of game plans from his assistant coaches: Are the plans really done up without his participation?

"If I had young coaches, I would spend more time coaching the coaches," he said. "But we have men with experience . . . they know what we want, and they have proved their capabilities over the years. I'll check a game plan and ask a question, just to let them know I'm aware of what they're doing, but I have confidence in them . . . it wouldn't work if I didn't."

You can find a fair number of people within the National Football League who will chuckle indulgently whenever terms like "practice" and "training camp" are used in the same breath with the Vikings.

The Minnesota attitude toward both of those necessities is couched in a basic Grant belief.

"Do what needs to be done . . . get it done, and then don't burden yourself with busywork."

"When you practice football, what's the point in running a play over and over again, after you've got it down? These men have been playing football for a long time . . . they know the game. I'd rather shorten the work period and preserve their concentration and energy for the game, when you know they'll need it."

The average NFL team spends about three weeks in two-a-day practices before it plays a preseason game. Grant's Vikings were there for a week . . . well, almost a week.

"This isn't original," he said, "but time spent doesn't represent work. I think someone said that back in about 1000 B.C.

"One of the biggest aspects of coaching is recognizing talent. We're confident we can go to training camp and pick out the football players. We don't need x number of scrimmages, we don't need to keep reexamining film minutely. We have utter confidence that we can watch a player in practice and evaluate him accurately . . . and when I say 'we,' I'm referring to our coaching staff as a whole."

The training camp period may be brief, but the work is not only concentrated, it is vital. There is a premium placed on practice performance . . . the Viking veterans knew that going in, but for rookies it can come as a shock.

Some years ago, the Vikings drafted an Ohio State fullback named Champ Henson . . . a big fellow, he'd had a big reputation in college.

He never played a down in a game for Minnesota.

"He asked me why," Grant recalled. "I told him he hadn't done the one thing he had to do and that was to demonstrate on the practice field that he belonged in a game. I told him I couldn't play him, based on what I'd seen . . . I didn't want to embarrass him, I didn't want to embarrass the team. The right to play doesn't come with any guarantee, you have to earn it, and the place you earn it is on the practice field."

Henson's father confronted Grant when his son was cut from the squad.

"He was very upset," said Bud. "He said it was inconceivable, or something like that, that his son couldn't play in the National Football League, after all he'd done at Ohio State.

"I told him I couldn't speak for the whole National Football League . . . I just knew he couldn't play for the Minnesota Vikings." Grant was right . . . Henson tried elsewhere after being cut at Minnesota. He never made it in the National Football League.

"We players heard all the stories about Bud when he came to Minnesota," recalled Paul Krause. "We heard that he'd hated practice when he was a player. I think he knew how we felt about practice . . . players realize practice is necessary, but that doesn't mean they like it. Bud's way was to get the work done and then get out of there."

Being on the practice field holds a certain appeal for Grant: "You see players up close, as they really are . . . without the trappings and circumstance of a game."

"He sees the little things that go into a person's makeup," said Tarkenton. "A man's got to demonstate his attitude and his ability on the practice field, and Bud doesn't miss much."

"He was so damned observant," said fullback Bill Brown. "Because he never gets excited, he wouldn't miss a trick. I don't mean he couldn't get upset if we were screwing up, but he could do it without losing his place. Most coaches, when they start to get mad, they lose their prospective. Bud never did that . . . he always kept things in their proper order."

"I know people criticized our training camps because they were shorter than most teams'," said Grant. "We wanted to come out of training camp with enthusiasm . . . not stagger out of it, exhausted. You go from training camp into the season . . . the season is why we're in business. We want our players to be excited when it starts, not tired."

Short as Grant's training camps were, there was always time for the boccie ball tournament . . . boccie is Italian lawn bowling. Nearly everybody participated. The tournament was marked by a high level of interest, lively betting on the side, and an unusually low level of sportsmanship. Grant and Krause, the safetyman, were camp champions for a number of years.

"I think we're similar, really," said Krause. "We both are low-key people, but we always want to win . . . I hate to lose at anything. It was exciting for me . . . Bud was always the coach, but when we played boccie, he was right on my level, out there battling with me."

Were there lessons to be learned on the boccie lawn?

"You learn that some people never win when the score is close," said Grant, "and some people always do."

8

The Winning Years

From 1969 through the 1971 season, the Vikings won thirty-five games and lost only seven. Their 1970 and 1971 postseason hopes were quashed early on, however. . . . San Francisco eliminated them in the first round of the 1970 playoffs, 17–14, and Dallas ousted them in the opening round in 1971, 20–12.

No matter . . . Finks reshuffled the personnel cards after the loss to Dallas, and Minnesota moved toward the 1972 season with renewed optimism. Tarkenton came back from New York in a trade, and the draft was a rich one with linebacker Jeff Siemon, running back Ed Marinaro . . . seen as Patrolman Joe Coffey on *Hill Street Blues* . . . and guard Charles Goodrum. Then, to assure success and provide Tarkenton with a target, Finks traded for John Gilliam, the fleet wide receiver from St. Louis.

The offensive retooling, set against the familiar excellence of the Viking defense, promised the best season yet.

It turned out to be one of the most disappointing . . . the Vikings finished 7–7, losing 20–17 at San Francisco in the final game. That game was the season in miniature . . . they ran to an early lead, only to falter under the weight of their own mistakes. John Brodie, the old pro, came off the bench late to win it for the 49ers.

After the game, in a somber dressing room, the light of anger danced in Grant's eyes.

"You'd better take a look at yourselves and see if you intend to play football next year, because this isn't going to happen again."

And it didn't . . . over the next six seasons, 1973 through 1978, the Vikings won six NFC Central Division titles, and in three of those years they won the conference title. Their record during that period was 62–22–2.

That run of success pretty much corresponded with the playing career of running back Chuck Foreman, whose chemistry together with Tarkenton's brought a drastic reshaping to the Viking offense.

Through the early years, Grant and the Vikings had won with relentless defensive pressure and an offense schooled in avoiding costly mistakes and turnovers. Grant's choice? More like Grant's analysis of the weapons at hand. The Vikings premiere players were on the defensive side of the ball, but with the return of Tarkenton and the acquisition of Gilliam and Foreman, the emphasis in talent shifted.

Tarkenton says he brought the passing game with him from New York and then refined it with Jerry Burns.

"But to give the devil his due," Francis quickly added, "Norm Van Brocklin had given me an understanding of the passing game before I left Minnesota."

Sir Francis warmed to his subject. "The thing is," he said, "most people are afraid of the passing game. That, and the fact that they don't understand it.

"Joe Montana's not that much better than some of the other passers, but the 49ers have a good scheme, and he understands it. More important, Bill Walsh understands it. You take a look at Walsh . . . he went to Cincinnati, and all of a sudden Greg Cook was the best passer in the AFC as a rookie. And we hadn't heard much about Greg Cook. Then he took Kenny Anderson and made him into an absolutely dynamite passer. He left Cincinnati and went to San Diego . . . that's when Dan Fouts went from being a young guy with promise to a great passer. When he got to San Francisco, he made Steve DeBerg a good quarterback, and then he got Montana and you know the rest of it.

"When I went to New York, I worked with Y. A. Tittle and Joe Walton, who is a super offensive coach, and we developed a passing game that was totally different. We utilized short passes, and for a simple reason . . . we didn't have a running game."

What was different about it?

"Teaching the quarterback to read a defense fast and always having someone to dump the ball off to instead of taking a loss. If you've got a good passing game, you don't require your quarterback to make great throws . . . that puts too much pressure on your offensive line. A 20-yard sideline pass is pretty, but you've got to throw the doggoned ball 40 to 45 yards to get it there! That means you've got to have great protection and a cannon for an arm. More often than not, a play like that just puts too much strain on your scheme."

Returning to the Vikings in 1972, Tarkenton brought his passing plan with him.

"I spent time with Burnsie [offensive coordinator Jerry Burns]. Within reason, I would say I had carte blanche to make suggestions.

You see, it can really be pretty simple if you'll just let it be simple. I had one read on a play . . . I read the middle linebacker or an outside backer or a safety, depending on what we had on. But after one read I knew exactly where I was going with the ball."

Tarkenton laughed.

"The problem is, people are afraid to make the darned passing game too simple. I got asked over to the University of Georgia to see if I couldn't help them with what they were doing. I watched and sat in their meetings, and finally I told Vince Dooley. I said, 'Vince, if you had Don Hutson and Sammy Baugh, you couldn't complete a pass . . . it's too darned complicated!'

"The system helped in Minnesota, but another thing that made it work was Bud . . . he doesn't get hung up on the numbers like a lot of coaches do. Bud doesn't care what you run a 40-yard dash in . . . he's in the football business, not a track coach. Chuck Foreman probably couldn't have played if you'd taken him on straight numbers, but he played fast. That's the key, people who can do it on Sunday," said Tarkenton.

"For five years, there wasn't a better back in football than Foreman," said Grant. "He was an outstanding pass receiver, and once he had the ball he was a great runner. And he had the ability to run the ball from scrimmage. He gave us different ways of attacking a defense."

The one-back offense has gained acclaim as a recent innovation . . . the Vikings were using it in the early seventies.

"Purple formation," Tarkenton confirmed. "We'd have Chuck as the single back or flank him out. Sometimes, we set Sammy White up as the back."

"Francis excelled at taking what was available," said Grant. "He made maximum use of Chuck Foreman. Francis read coverages beautifully, and he was a master at making something out of a bad situation. If the coverage wasn't what we'd anticipated and the pattern he wanted wasn't up, he'd dump the ball off to Foreman. Francis wasn't as interested in backs who could pick up the blitz as in backs he could throw to. He didn't like to waste plays."

Talking about Foreman, Grant explained his theory on football's aging process.

"Chuck played very well for five years, probably about as long as he should have. Today, we have Walter Payton in Chicago, but he's a rarity . . . most backs don't play past thirty. Some of the big backs . . . people like Brown and Ollie Matson . . . played longer, but they were bigger. Chuck wasn't a power-runner type, although he weighed about 210. The big, power-running back matures later . . . the smaller man, who relies on his speed and elusiveness, plays his best football in his first five seasons."

Grant on Tarkenton?

"I don't think there has been a quarterback who can measure up to him," said Bud. "The remarkable thing is he went out on top. He played eighteen years, and I think he threw twenty-five touchdown passes in his last season. Unitas, Starr, Namath, Bradshaw . . . it was different for them when they were near the end.

"The first thing about Francis was his intelligence. He is an inquisitive person, and he was interested in the broad scope of things, not just his job. He's a great visitor . . . he loved to sit and talk about football or about anything. When he first came back, he offered advice a few times on trades, but we got that straightened out."

Bud believes Tarkenton wouldn't have played as long as he did, had he not been a quarterback. "Football wouldn't have been that challenging to him if he had been a position player," said Bud. "I don't think he could have kept his concentration."

Tarkenton on the same subject:

"He prolonged my interest, and because he did, he prolonged my career."

Grant's response to those who see Tarkenton as being too glib?

"I think it's a facade. He likes to talk, he's good at it, and he has had a lot of public exposure. Francis has a way of managing any situation he's in. But he also has depth . . . we have talked many times over the years, and not all about football. He's never had a facade around me."

"I was tickled to death to play for Bud," said Tarkenton. "If you can't play for Bud Grant, you can't play.

"It amazes me . . . always will . . . how he just flat makes sense.

"He told me once it isn't the talent level that keeps a rookie from playing so often, it's because he has so many things on his mind that his concentration suffers. And they were little things . . . where you shop, how you get around in a new town, who does your laundry, where should you bank. A veteran's got all that down, so he frees his mind up. The result is, the rookie's not comfortable yet, and the veteran is. When he said that, I remember saying to myself, 'That really makes sense, and it's so simple. Why in the heck didn't I think of that?'

"I say Bud didn't coach much, but in his special way, he did.

"We could have a situation where I was wanting to throw the football, and he could talk me out of it without ever telling me not to."

How did he do it?

"Say we were at our own 40, up by 7 points, looking at third and 8. I'd go over to the bench during a time-out, and old Bud would say, 'Well, we've got a 7-point lead, there's not much time left, and our defense has been stuffin' them.' That's all he'd say, but that was enough . . . I knew I wasn't supposed to put it up. He didn't tell me to run the football, but he did tell me . . . he established the parameters of logic for my decision."

Grant, said Tarkenton, is not a "diseased football fanatic. He doesn't like to lose, but if you lose, it's not the end-all. He is a great leader if you accept the definition that a leader is one who inspires others to do their job well. He does that as well as any leader I've ever been associated with. He proves, very refreshingly, that you can be a great leader and coach, and still have your life together.

"I miss being around his logic," Tarkenton concluded.

Kapp, the quarterback, has received mention as an important Viking, and he was. But Joe had this transient quality to him . . . he wasn't for the long haul. He was more like a fierce wind blowing across your property . . . leaving sign of its passage, but then moving on.

But there were Vikings for the long haul, like Tarkenton . . . and the coach with the uncluttered philosophy built on them.

Grady Alderman was a bright fellow who divided his time between playing offensive tackle and working as a tax accountant. He was small by today's standards . . . about 240 pounds and he stood 6-foot-2.

"Durable," said Grant of Alderman. "Durable" is one of Bud Grant's favorite words. "Durable" football players are Grant's favorite kind . . . abiding, enduring men who use the mortar of perseverance to bind the bricks of talent and enthusiasm.

"This is a profession," said Grant, "a job. The durable player takes pride in his profession. He accepts his responsibilities on the good days, when he feels like it, and on the bad days, when he doesn't. It's a business where durable people earn the benefits. Football, as a short-term investment of your time and energies, would be a poor investment. You'd be better off in something else."

A West Coast writer, analyzing the Vikings during their glory years, wrote of Grady Alderman:

"He has good mobility, and that permits him to maintain contact with the defensive end. Eventually, the end will overpower him, because of his size. Unfortunately, that never seems to happen until just after the Viking passer has thrown the ball."

"Grady knew his position," said Grant. "He also knew what he was capable of, and he had discipline."

In 1961, the late George Halas had a surplus of fullbacks at Chicago . . . he had respected veterans Rick Casares and Joe Marconi, and a brash young rookie from Illinois named Bill Brown.

Halas traded Brown to the Vikings, over the protests of another brash young Bear rookie, tight end Mike Ditka.

"I told him, 'Coach, I know it's not my business, but we oughta keep Brown.' I was right . . . it wasn't my business. But there's tough, and then there's really tough, and Billy was really tough. Plus, he was a super athlete," said Ditka.

In support of Mike's theory, Halas ran into Brown's wife, Kay, several years later, following a Bears–Vikings game in Minnesota. Halas wasn't coaching them. He rode down in the postgame elevator, saw Kay, and made a courtly bow to her.

"Young lady," he said, "I am George Halas. I want you to know that trading your husband away was the worst mistake I ever made as coach of the Chicago Bears."

The fans called him Boom-Boom.

Herb Adderley, who played cornerback for Green Bay with distinction, once wailed in frustration on the Packer sideline after futile attempts to stop the low-slung Viking fullback.

"He's got no handles on him," roared Adderley. "It's like trying to tackle a goddamned bowling ball!"

"It's probably wrong to say that one player was the best," said Grant, "but, for a time, Bill Brown was the epitome of the Vikings. He asked no quarter, and he gave none." For years, Brown teamed in the Viking backfield with Dave Osborn, a North Dakota farmboy with a high, piping voice. The two were simplistic . . . they simply loved to play football, and they played every down as though it would be their last.

"Wayne Walker played linebacker for Detroit then," Grant recalled, "and I can remember him saying how he hated to play against us because of Brown and Osborn. He said it didn't matter which one of them was carrying the ball, he knew both of them were going to hit him their best lick on every play."

Bill Brown bought Grant's program . . . indeed, he was an easy sell.

"He liked it, he liked all of it," said Grant. "Bill liked playing in the cold weather, he liked working hard in practice, he liked doing whatever was required for us to win."

No matter how cold the day, when the Vikings took the field for pregame warm-ups, Brown would have his sleeves rolled up and refuse to wear a jacket. He also refused to pad his arms or elbows, so he was always a mass of scabs and bruises.

"Once before a game, I watched him knocking scabs off his elbows," said Grant. "The blood was running down his arms. I asked him why he did it. 'To get ready,' was what he answered. Players on the other team could see him doing that, too . . . they got the message."

"I guess some people had trouble with Bud," said Brown, "but I didn't. He didn't mess with you . . . anything Bud gave you had a reason, it was something that would help you."

Brown's variation on why Bud Grant succeeded as a football coach?

"He was very fair. He didn't try to restrict you, but at the same time, you operated within his system. He was very orderly, he never rushed into things.

"I suppose if he taught us anything, it was that moderation makes sense. That's Bud's life-style, really, moderation . . . not letting anything overwhelm you. Sometimes, as a player, you can get things around to where football looks like life or death. It isn't, but you can screw yourself up to where you think it is. Bud never did, though. And he was good at letting you know that if you played as hard as you could, that was all you could do . . . you weren't gonna die from it.

"I think his rule of thumb was a fair one," said Brown. "If you were durable and if you were consistent, you'd play. I think he's that way with his coaches, too . . . he's fair with them. I saw Steckel override his coaches that year he was here, and it can be disastrous. Bud would never do that."

Grant called Brown a total contributor to the team. "When he was over thirty and wasn't able to play regularly as a running back, he was captain of the special teams."

Bill Brown is loud, brash, funny, and kind. He wore a crew cut long before he met Grant and still wears one. He laughs harder at himself than he does at others. His voice, such as it is, sounds like gravel being swished around in the bottom of a tin pail.

And every football team should have forty just like him.

"He was the Vikings," said Grant.

Osborn, Brown's running mate, had been scouted by Grant as a collegian when Bud was still in Canada.

"The only thing I knew for sure about Ozzie when I got to Minnesota was that he could not catch a football," said Bud. "You see good receivers and fair receivers and poor receivers, but still they are people who can take the ball into their hands. Ozzie couldn't.

"I told him if he was going to play, he had to learn how to catch the football. That was all he needed to hear. He just overwhelmed his problem with work . . . he practiced and practiced and practiced until he could catch the ball. It wasn't pretty . . . he'd box it or grab it against his chest, but he'd catch it. We were at Detroit once," Grant recalled, "and Ozzie was running scot-free behind their secondary. He was wide open. I saw the ball in the air, for him, and I died a thousand deaths, watching. He spun one way, then the other . . . he almost fell down, but he caught it. Ozzie could make a routine catch look spectacular."

If Grant had concerns with Osborn's catching skills, he didn't go public with them.

"Bud never criticized you publicly or even in front of the other players," said Osborn. "He didn't believe in embarrassing people. As a result, he got maximum effort out of players and their respect, too.

"He was honest . . . positive but honest," Osborn added. "I can remember him talking to us before a game and saying, 'Now, they're better than we are . . . but that doesn't mean we don't have a chance to win, provided we play smart.' Because he was realistic, he made us look at things realistically. And honest . . . I believe he'd cut his own son if he thought it would help the team."

Osborn spoke of Grant's even-keeled approach . . . the avoidance of highs and lows.

"He'd tell us that to be pro athletes, we had to be self-motivated. He didn't want a guy he'd have to kick in the butt, just as he didn't want somebody to be sky-high. He wanted you to play intelligently, to play within your ability, and to take advantage of the other team's mistakes.

"You know, we didn't have a lot of stars," Osborn pointed out. "I mean, we had some good players, but most of the guys on our team, me included, looked like they should have been playing a pickup game at the church picnic instead of in the NFL. He said it was more important that we have intelligence and durability and that we play consistently. I think consistency was important to Bud because he had to know what to expect from a player . . . he didn't want some guy who'd be all-world one week, then out to lunch the next.

"Bud's the kind of person who appealed to me," said Osborn. "I guess we're kind of alike in that we don't make a lot of whoop-de-la. I've always been a striver. I think, from Bud, I learned that there's no easy way . . . if there was, everybody would be a winner. You must have desire, and you must be willing to work."

Grant says Osborn had one gift he has never seen in another athlete.

"He could will himself to run faster," said Bud. "He's the only person I've seen who could do that. What I mean is, running what should be your fastest and then being able to run even faster. He did it in games, he did it in practice. We drafted Clinton Jones, and we knew that Clinton was faster than Ozzie. Yet, whenever they would run a match race at 40 yards, Clinton never could beat him. Dave Osborn thrived on competition."

It was noted that Bill Brown bought Grant's program. If Brown made that purchase for the Vikings offense, defensive end Jim Marshall made it for the defense.

Captain Jim.

He played end, and he was the consummate professional. He stood 6-foot-3 and seldom weighed more than 240 pounds. Sometimes, he weighed less than 230. It didn't matter. Jim Marshall was as swift and nimble and sure as a stalking cat, and absolutely oblivious to pain.

"We couldn't have made it without Jim," said Grant.

"Jim bought the program, but never from an Uncle Tom standpoint. He didn't try to cozy up to me. He never sought special treatment, nor did he receive it. If we needed to do something, Jim would say, 'Okay, Boss,' and he would set the pace. Younger players would be forced to look at Jim and say, 'If he does it, who won't do it?'

"There is such a shock factor for a lot of people coming into pro football," said Grant. "They come from a college program where they were a star . . . they are accustomed to lining up across from somebody . . . from anybody . . . and knowing they're better than that man. They think it's going to be that way in the pros, too. But they get into camp, and they line up against some old guy who's not as big as they are, and he's got gray in his hair, and suddenly they realize this old guy is just beating the hell out of them. It's a terrible shock. They are forced to admit to themselves that some old man is killing them.

"That happens," Grant went on, "because they are up against a true professional. That's what Jim Marshall was, and I have a very special feeling for him."

During the upheaval of a player strike, Viking defensive tackle Alan Page was a visible foe of management.

"Alan was going to walk out," said Grant. "Jim Marshall talked to me about it. He said Alan shouldn't go alone . . . he said if he went with him, it wouldn't seem like such a big deal. He was right . . . he usually was."

Jim Marshall played in 282 consecutive games, more than any man in the history of the National Football League. And he played them down and dirty, on the line of scrimmage . . . a truly remarkable achievement.

Page, in his prime, very well may have played the game better than any man in NFL history. He remains the only defensive player ever named Most Valuable Player of the league. He was devastating.

Chuck Knox, the coach, talked once about preparing to meet the Vikings when he coached the Los Angeles Rams.

"I watched this film," said Knox, "and I kept running one play over and over. Page made three definite mistakes after the ball was snapped, and still made the tackle for no gain."

The Grant–Page relationship went full circle, from Page's being named MVP of the league in 1971 to Grant's decision to put him on waivers during the 1978 season.

"He asked me if I didn't think he could play anymore," said Grant. "I told him I knew he could still play, it just wouldn't be here."

Mick Tingelhoff, a free agent from Nebraska, played seventeen years and 240 games at center for the Vikings.

"He would have been an All-Pro as a linebacker, too," said Grant, "he had that personality. 'Deadly' would be the word to describe the way Mick played.

"Mick liked the tough part of football . . . the rougher it got, the closer the score, the bigger the stakes . . . that's when he was happiest. Nobody on that team . . . and I mean nobody . . . would have dreamed of messing with Mick."

Grant told a story to make his point.

"I was leaving the parking lot after a game at the old Met, and Mick was right in front of me in his pickup. There was only one exit lane from the area we parked in, so you just had to line up and go slow and wait your turn. It worked, you just had to be patient.

"We were waiting in line, when these guys in a car came gunning down the outside and tried to cut into the lane, right in front of Mick. They were honking and pointing and shouting, but Mick just shook his head . . . I guess he figured they could wait in line like the rest of us.

"Well, pretty soon the three guys pile out of their car and go for Mick. I remember thinking, 'You shouldn't do that.'

"Mick got out of his truck, and it was just pop, pop, pop . . . he threw three little short punches, and the three of them were on the ground. Then Mick got back in his truck and drove on."

Mick Tingelhoff laughed that low, slow laugh of his when he was reminded of the incident. And then he talked about Grant.

"I remember the player strike, back in 1970. I was the Viking player rep. I went in to see Bud . . . I had to tell him I didn't think the veterans would be reporting for training camp. It was a bad time, everybody was mad, and there had been a lot written and said. I wasn't looking forward to going in to Bud. Well, I told him what I had to tell him, and he never changed expression. After a while, he said, 'Don't worry about it. From what I know of strikes, they end when they're supposed to end.' He was right, and he was able to keep from getting all emotional about it."

Why is Grant successful?

"He thinks things through," said Tingelhoff. "He doesn't rush and then make stupid statements he has to be sorry for. I think I'm a little bit like him, kind of laid-back. He taught me never to worry about the things you can't control.

"People say he's a cold guy," Tingelhoff went on. "He's not cold, he's just got things figured out a lot better than the rest of us."

Mick laughed. "You know, he can say more with his eyes than most people can by speaking.

"I admire him, and I consider him a friend. I guess I admire the way he's lived . . . he's done exactly what he wanted to do, and not many of us can say that.

"I think about him a lot," said Tingelhoff. "I'll be out hunting, tramping a field, and I'll find myself thinking about Bud."

Eller, the defensive end, spoke of how, for him, Grant was difficult to get used to.

"I was used to a coach having more interaction with players, whether positive or negative. With Bud, it was more a hands-off policy, and that made it difficult for me. Bud was so even-tempered . . . he didn't upstage a player, and he left the emotions of the game for us. After a while, I came to appreciate his way. He forced some of us to take a leadership role within the team, to see that everybody was together.

"I think Bud won because of his calm," said Eller. "He made the right choice so often in very emotional situations because of that calm. He is a very sensitive and perceptive person . . . he's got a real gift for knowing exactly how far he can go in a situation."

Was Grant a coach, as well as a person?

"He'd tell you to watch for something in a situation . . . maybe just one little thing. But it made an impression. You knew it was coming from his knowledge. And every time he'd cover something, it would be a thing the assistant coaches hadn't mentioned. But Bud's coaching had more to do with objectives than technique."

Eller watched, along with the rest of Minnesota, as Grant left football and then returned.

"He doesn't change," said the Moose. "People here have him in very high esteem, but he's still Bud, and he's not about to lose that. He has an identity of self, and that's a real important lesson."

All this talk about even keels, self-identity, and the like is not without purpose . . . Grant needed it for his stewardship of a set of linebackers whose life-style collided spectacularly with his own. Roy Winston, Lonnie Warwick, and Wally Hilgenberg were musketeers in purple helmets.

Between them, they circled all of Grant's least favorite bases with aplomb . . . smoking, drinking, and raising hell. To equate with baseball, linebackers are at the heart of a defensive team's batting order. They would bat three, four, and five. And they took their cuts with gusto, both on and off the field.

How in the world did Bud Grant ever identify with them?

"By appealing to their intelligence," Grant replied.

"The one thing about those fellows, they were all extremely intelligent. Hell-raisers, yes, but the other thing they had in common was the ability to think.

"Lonnie Warwick's education wasn't all that great, but he was a very bright guy. The same with Roy and Wally, they weren't at all slow. You can go to some players and give them logic, and they can't follow you at all. These three could and did. And I don't think they had ever been treated that way before . . . they had always been treated as animals."

Played like them, too . . . with some frequency.

Roy Winston was the smallest of the animals, a square-rigged 225-pounder who stood a shade under 5-foot-11.

He was an excellent football player.

When Grant arrived in Minnesota, Roy was talented, undisciplined, and moody. He had his problems accepting Grant's program . . . up to a point.

Bud remembers the point well.

"Roy came to a team meeting, and he'd been drinking quite a bit," said Grant. "He was loud. This was close to Roy's transitional time as a player . . . he still had good years left, but he wasn't a kid any longer.

"Anyway, he was causing a commotion, so I asked him to go out in the hall with me. He hollered something like 'Fine, go ahead and get rid of me, I don't want to be here, anyhow!'

"I told him he wasn't in any shape to attend a meeting and that he should go to his room in the dorm. He called me just about every name in the book, but he finally went to his room. I told him I'd talk to him later.

"He was at my door at seven the next morning," Grant recalled. "He stood there, frowning, and said all he wanted to know was how much it was going to cost him. I told him, and he said, 'That's fine.' I think it was very difficult for Roy to say he was sorry, but in his way, he did. He was never a problem after that.

"Roy was having a difficult time," Grant explained. "He was trying to decide whether he could accept our type of football. After that incident he did, and he came to enjoy it. And he was a major contributor."

Indeed, Grant's disciplined football suited Roy Winston perfectly. Another team, given more to preconceived physical standards, would have marked Winston down as "too short" and been done with it. But as Tarkenton had suggested, Grant was more interested in people who played well than in those who looked good on a computer printout. And Winston played very well.

"Roy worked hard," said Bud, "and he went from being a hard-drinking, bullying, raucous kind of guy to being a very intense, disciplined player."

He bought the program?

"He did, but I don't want to make it sound like it was that easy for him or that I really had a program or a timetable for players. It just

happened. It isn't that I set out to change Roy Winston or any player
. . . it was up to him, it was his decision, not mine."

The linebacker who once cussed Grant out in a hallway outside a
meeting room now greets him with a bear hug and tears in his eyes
when their paths cross.

"He's a friend of mine," said Grant. "Roy is a good example of a
man who got everything out of football."

What made Grant a great coach? Roy Winston was asked.

"I think, just the man himself," said Winston. "You know, he
used to preach to us about making the big play . . . he did it so much,
we got to where we believed in it just like he did. We might be down
. . . Lord, there were a lot of times when we were down . . . but we
believed an opportunity would present itself, and we knew that if we
seized it, we would have a chance to win."

Winston spoke of Grant's knack for seeing seemingly insignificant
incidents on the practice field and recognizing their importance.

"He'd shut down the whole practice for a play if he saw us do
something wrong, when he knew it was important. He'd stop everything and explain. It was just one play, but he'd know it was the play
that might win for us."

And he spoke of Grant's memory.

"We were playing Pittsburgh in the Super Bowl and Bradshaw
came on a rollout, down near the goal line. I was coming on a blitz,
but Franco Harris picked me up. I went down, then got up to chase,
but it was too late. The next summer, in training camp, the same
darned play came up. Bud saw it right away and reminded me how, if
I'd contained in the Super Bowl, Bradshaw wouldn't have gotten in."

Winston echoed the thoughts of his teammates when he talked
about his memories of Grant.

"He was so patient . . . he didn't make decisions until they had to
be made. I've tried to learn that from him, except my wife just says
it's procrastinating."

Told that Grant's wife had leveled a similar charge against him,
Winston laughed.

"Yeah," he said, "but when Bud did it, we won football games because of it. He took the time to make the right decision."

Bud Grant . . . conservative, deliberate, methodical, wary.

Right?

It depends.

Back a ways, the Vikings were at New Orleans, in a game they
very much needed to win. They had, however, spent the first half
being buffeted by a fired-up Saints squad. And when the two teams
came back out to start the second half, New Orleans smelled blood.

But only briefly.

Grant called for an onside kickoff to open the second half . . . the Vikings recovered, and all of the air went out of the Saints' balloon.

Beneath that frosty countenance, there is a side to Grant that embraces the unusual with enthusiasm.

"Providing," Grant qualified, "that the situation is right.

"We played the Jets once, and they pulled a fake field goal that went for a touchdown, but the point was they already had the game in hand. There was no element of risk, no gamble . . . nothing to be gained from it. It shouldn't be an ego trip . . . if you've got a card to play, you save it for the right occasion.

"And it's like cards," Grant added. "If you're going to bluff, make sure there's a big pot."

Dave Osborn referred to Grant as "chairman of the board" on the sidelines during a game . . . and well-said. There's no conference table or pin-striped suits, but Bud's definitely in charge.

Grant was asked if the Vikings "scripted" their offensive plays, in the manner attributed to Bill Walsh, the astute coach of the San Francisco 49ers. Lore has it that Walsh prepares a list of plays he feels will work against the day's opponent, and then methodically runs them as the game unfolds.

Grant accepts this philosophy with a dash of salt.

"We've never seen the list, have we?" he said.

"I'm sure Bill is like the rest of us, in that he works on things he feels will be good against an opponent and wants to utilize them. But down and distance influence situations . . . in our case, we're interested in judging defensive reaction. We'll try to show the formations we have in for a game in the first few series so that we can judge the defensive reaction. Of course, if we've got a surprise in mind for later, we'll save that.

"That lets us know what formations have the best chance of succeeding."

Once the game begins, Grant clamps on his headset over a purple cap and takes his stand on the sidelines, arms folded . . . he seems detached from the usual hubbub of the bench.

What's he doing?

Listening, for one thing. His headset links him with Burns, the offensive coordinator, who is in an observation booth upstairs along with the defensive spotter coaches. Jerry Burns is very bright and very gifted . . . he also has, in game situations, language that would make a sailor blush.

"It's been so many years now," Grant mused. "I just kind of sort it out from the stuff I need to hear."

He grinned. "I've had two major failures over the years . . . I couldn't get Bill Brown to quit smoking, and I couldn't get Burnsie to clean up his language."

Grant's headset permits him to listen to the offensive coaches, to the defensive coaches, to the special team coaches, and to the player phone on the sideline.

"I might be up on the sideline, watching play and talking on the phone to a player who's twenty feet behind me," he said.

"The big thing is I want to know what's being said. If a player tells his position coach something, I want to know it. Maybe a receiver will come out after a play and say the corner's playing way out on his outside shoulder. I want to know that . . . we've got things we can do to take advantage of that. If a substitution is going to be made, I want to be aware of it."

Grant is puzzled by some coaches who do not wear the headset and appear to walk the sideline cut off from the flow of communication.

"I don't know what they do," he said. "Even if another coach is calling the plays, I'd think they would want to be aware of the calls."

Grant is quietly irked by people who say they watch him on the sideline during a game and don't see him do anything.

"I'll guarantee you," he said, "I'm doing a lot more than just watching the game."

Unlike government, with its system of checks and balances, the politics of the sidelines are not so evenly weighted. Grant has the only veto.

Burns will call plays, but he calls them within the framework approved by Grant. Or Bud may tell the defensive coaches that he wants the front changed from four-man to three for the next series . . . then it's up to the coaches to make the arrangements.

The assistant coaches are the technicians, highly skilled in their area of responsibility.

"In no way do I know as much about offensive line play as John Michels," Grant explained. "I know something about people and about what it takes to play, but as far as what you can or can't do in a situation, or what's feasible against a certain team, there is no comparison of my knowledge to his. I respect his knowledge."

Another thing about Bud Grant football . . . emotion must share time with calm on the knife blade of purpose.

"Emotion is great," said Grant, "and we want as much of it as the players can muster. But it has to be directed properly. We don't want people screaming at each other or raving at the officials. Emotion is a tool, provided you use it properly. It's a source of energy. Like energy, it shouldn't be wasted."

The Vikings are notorious around the NFL for being late arrivers at the stadium on game day.

It is another example of Grant's conserving energy.

When Grant was a senior football player at the University of Minnesota, the Gophers went to Michigan for a key game. Because of the crush of fans at the team hotel, Minnesota coach Bernie Bierman took his squad to the stadium almost three hours before the game. The players fretted themselves up to and beyond the point of readiness . . . when they finally took the field, they were flat and lost the game.

While it may be only coincidence, Grant's Viking teams reach the stadium on a timetable that has them jumping into uniform at about the same pace firemen dress for a five-alarmer.

"We want to tie our shoes and walk out on the field," said Grant. "We do not want players sitting around the locker room in an emotional state."

Two of Minnesota's biggest playoff games involved the Dallas Cowboys . . . they won one and lost one.

The 1973 Vikings went to Texas Stadium to play for the National Football Conference championship and a Super Bowl berth. They won 27–10. Minnesota's play, particularly in the first half of that game, was awesome . . . Tarkenton, whether passing or directing traffic, may never have been better.

"Jerry Burns put in some things for that game that we hadn't shown before," Grant explained. "Dallas is a very key-conscious team. Jerry developed a set of false keys . . . he gave the Cowboys one look and then did something else. The result was we pretty much took LeRoy Jordan, the middle linebacker, out of the game. Dallas is such a programmed team that anytime you give them something they haven't seen, it bothers them. The same plays didn't work in the second half, of course, because they figured out where our people were coming from and made adjustments. The game wasn't won by halftime, but we had the upper hand."

In 1975, Dallas returned the favor, winning in the playoffs at Met Stadium on Roger Staubach's desperation "Hail Mary" pass to Drew Pearson.

"It's ironic, the way things turn out," said Grant. "The best football in that game was when we drove the ball to score and take the lead in the fourth quarter. It may have been the finest drive a Viking team has ever made, because it was a critical situation, we couldn't afford a mistake, and we had to score. We made all the plays against an excellent defense . . . had we won the game, that drive would have been the thing people remembered."

But they didn't win, and the drive paled alongside Staubach's shocking pass completion to Pearson.

With less than 30 seconds remaining, Dallas had second down at midfield. From the shotgun formation, Staubach pumped to hold safetyman Krause in the deep middle, and then hurled the ball deep, down the right side, for Pearson, covered man-for-man by Nate Wright.

"They knew what they had to do . . . take a chance," said Grant. "We knew it, too.

"Pearson pushed off Nate Wright on the play, but it was either their last chance or very close to it . . . what did they have to lose? The push was apparent, and there were two officials on the catch so, in that sense, we were victims.

"On the other hand," said Grant, "it was a great play. Pearson must have been a basketball player at some point, because that was a basketball play. He didn't push too soon . . . he waited until the ball was almost there, until he and Nate were both in the air. Then he pushed off, and Nate went on the ground. If he had pushed while they were still running, he wouldn't have knocked Nate off stride. But it was a remarkable play by Pearson . . . jump, push a man away, and catch the football, all in the same motion. It couldn't have been easy."

Grant's first NFL coaching victory came in his native Wisconsin, where he was matched against the fearsome, legendary Lombardi. One hundred and fifty regular season victories later, his team defeated the Cincinnati Bengals in the final game before Grant's one-year retirement . . . the Bengals were owned by Paul Brown, the man who had shown him the purpose of football, back at Great Lakes.

"I didn't know Lombardi well," Grant recalled. "But I had talked to him several times while I was at Winnipeg. The first conversation was about Fuzzy Thurston. He'd been cut by Baltimore, and we brought him to Canada because we needed a guard. He'd been there a day or two when Lombardi got hold of him. Fuzzy came in to see me. He said he realized he had signed a contract with us, but his heart was still in the NFL. He said he would really appreciate it if we would let him go, so he could get a chance with the Packers.

"We let him go," Grant said, "and he went on to become All-Pro at Green Bay."

Grant and Lombardi competed for one more player while Bud was at Winnipeg, a fellow named Dale Hackbart.

Hackbart had been a football and baseball star at Wisconsin. He was drafted in the NFL by Green Bay, but chose to sign a baseball contract instead.

"He was with a Northern League team, so he played in Winnipeg several times," Grant recalled. "The first time through, everything was fine, and he was happy with baseball. The next time, though, I visited with him before the last game of the series, and I could tell he was discouraged . . . he was an outfielder, and he was having trouble hitting professional pitching. Football was beginning to sound better to him.''

Grant watched the game. As he was driving home, he decided Hackbart might be ready to consider a football offer.

"I headed back to the park, but I got there just as their bus was leaving, heading back down to the States,'' said Bud.

Grant was called the Gray Fox in Canada, and the nickname was no accident.

"I called a fellow I knew who worked customs at the border,'' he said. "I told him to hold that bus until I got there.''

That was how he signed Dale Hackbart.

When it came time for Hackbart to report for practice at Winnipeg the following summer, Lombardi called Grant to say he wanted Hackbart in Green Bay.

"I told him, 'No way, you already stole Thurston from me,' '' said Grant.

Bud grinned. "You know Lombardi . . . first he talked nice, then he raised his voice, then he started hollering. I just listened. After a while, he said, 'What's it going to take?' I think it took fifteen thousand dollars . . . I know it was enough for us to go out and sign another American.''

Footnote to history: Hackbact was never a factor at Green Bay, but returned to play well for Grant, both at Winnipeg and Minnesota.

Bud Grant is in the business of living. One aspect of that business has been to serve as a football coach, and he has served well.

He reflected on the coaching part of it and its importance.

"A football game is very important at the time,'' he said, "but what is forgotten quicker than the outcome of a game? It isn't like being a doctor or a politician or an airplane pilot, where your decisions can impact permanently on the lives of people.

"It's an entertainment form for the people who watch us, and when it's over, they go about their business. With the exception of the next morning's newspaper, there isn't much left of it. That's because there's another game next week . . . and some people lose sight of that in our business. It's not entertainment for us, of course . . . it's a job. It pays well because the entertainment industry pays well, but its importance is not earth-shattering.''

Is that enough for Grant, being a part of the entertainment industry?

"It's extremely competitive,'' he said. "It draws competitive people to it, and an enjoyable aspect of the job is associating with competitive people.''

How can you call it entertainment when a center and a nose tackle are down there, slugging it out? Isn't it pretty desperate to them?

"It's hard work for them," he answered. "If you go up on the stage and rock-'n'-roll for three hours, that's hard work, too. People in the entertainment industry work harder than you think. I don't care if you're a football player or a singer or a race driver, there's a lot of hard work that goes into preparation. The fan only sees the finished product . . . the work that goes on behind the scenes is enormous."

Is there a take-away benefit for being the coach . . . a pleasure taken in seeing players develop?

"Not as much as if I had been a real teacher . . . a schoolteacher, say," Grant answered. "But there's a plus side. There are times when it's gratifying to see a fellow realize the achievements he is capable of. Unfortunately, I'm probably more aware of the negative side . . . the people who leave the game with a bitter feeling. Some players lose all of the good things that happened to them to bitterness.

"The time comes, for every player, when he can no longer perform his job to the level at which it must be performed. He doesn't want to quit, he wants to continue playing, but he can't . . . it's not an easy thing. A player will say he wants to go to camp for another year, but he doesn't want to do all of that work and run the risk of being cut. What he really wants is a guarantee, and you can't give him one. I have seen men leave the game at that point with bitterness, because they couldn't accept the fact that it was their time. And that is the feeling that remains with them, even though they had some wonderful experiences in sport.

"That bothers me."

Grant remembered attending a NFL coaches' meeting when he first went to Minnesota. He spent time with three fellow head coaches: Tom Fears, Norb Hecker, and Bill Austin.

"I felt like a real dunce, listening to them," Bud said. "They knew exactly what strategy they would use. They had everything down pat. I went away from that meeting feeling very inadequate, because I had no idea who would start for us or what we'd end up using."

If this story has a moral, it is that Fears, Hecker, and Austin are long since departed from the head coaching fraternity.

"I think about that," Grant said. "Maybe, the key is, you have to remain flexible. Once at Winnipeg, before we started training camp, I made a list of those players I thought would be starters for us during the coming season. Then I put the list in my drawer. I looked at it after the season . . . it didn't bear much resemblance to what had really happened.

"That struck me as a good thing to remember," said Grant.

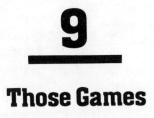

9

Those Games

There's a story about a fellow who, in search of new experiences, jumped onto a cactus plant.

He was lying there, all full of cactus needles and hurting, when a friend of his came by.

"Why in the world did you do that?" the friend asked.

"I don't know," the fellow groaned. "It seemed like it was worth trying at the time."

Which is one way to approach the Vikings' four journeys to Super Bowl.

They went to Super Bowl IV and lost 23–7 to Kansas City. They faced Miami in VIII and lost 24–7. It was Pittsburgh in IX, 16–6. Their last try was against the then Oakland Raiders in XI, and the score was 32–14, with Oakland on top.

Incredible, right?

This durable, resourceful, disciplined team with its durable, resourceful, disciplined coach scaled the sheer wall of the playoffs four times, only to find the banana peel on each occasion in the final, fateful step.

Incredible, wrong.

The Vikings were beaten, convincingly, in those games by teams which were better, at least on those days, than they were.

Why?

"Journalists try to explain things," said Grant. "I don't. I've never tried to explain those games to myself or to anybody else. We got beat. We did as well as we could, but we got beat. I don't feel any stigma.

"Those games are like any sporting event, a part of the record. The score remains. You deal with the record, not with how each score was achieved. I don't think we were scarred by those games . . . after each of them, we came back to win our division the next year."

Of the four losses, Grant cited the Oakland game as the one that got out of hand quickly. "They really played well . . . Stabler was as good that day as we've seen him."

In Super Bowl VIII, against Miami in Rice Stadium in Houston, Grant drew media attention and NFL fire when he took public exception to his team's spartan practice facilities. He didn't make a big thing out of the fact that the players had to hang their clothes on nails, but he did express some reservations about a sparrow in the shower room.

Criticism from within isn't a real big seller at Super Bowl. There were suggestions, from that same direction, that Grant, an avowed naturalist, might have imported the sparrow from Minnesota.

Now, if you're looking for a good way to lose the handle on Grant, ramming party lines down his throat seems like a good place to start. He is as comfortable in that posture as a Wyoming bronco would be in a string of Central Park riding horses.

And he swears he didn't bring the sparrow with him.

"You've got to have something to talk about besides the matchup at center," he explained. "You're asked to make a lot of statements . . . and a lot of it is just words. You can't say, 'I don't know,' or 'I don't care.' But a lot of what you are asked has very little to do with the game."

Grant felt the other Super Bowl games presented Minnesota with opportunities. "We were in them longer or the margin was deceptive because of some things that happened. But what happened, happened . . . to say anything more would be sour grapes. That's the intriguing part of this business . . . you don't know how it's going to turn out."

Would you like to go back?

"Sure . . . we might win four in a row."

Grant has been criticized for his matter-of-fact approach to the Super Bowl. Again, people within the industry have writhed at suggestions that it is "another game." Grant has been frowned upon the way an interloper at a royal court would be if he were to suggest that he was going to wear his clothes to the grand ball.

Bud's point is, his work clothes were what got him here in the first place.

"The Super Bowl is just another game . . . a game with interruptions," Grant clarified. "The interruptions fit around what you do as a team. You can't practice twice as much or become twice as well-prepared, because it's Super Bowl. You still do the things that got you there."

Grant's strongest take-away from the Super Bowls has to do with endurance.

"There is an instant elation when you know you're going to play in the game, but then it becomes an endurance contest. The team that sustains itself, endures within the events leading to the game, has the best chance.''

Walsh, the San Francisco coach, spoke of losing the big one several days before his team won its first Super Bowl victory, over Cincinnati at Detroit. He felt the loser was treated unfairly.

"We have two teams that play so beautifully, just to get there,'' Walsh noted. "But the team that loses practically has to slink out of town. I think it's terribly unfair.''

Bud Grant doesn't agree.

"It may seem unfair, but it is an extension of the thing that made this country great,'' said Grant, "and that is the high acclaim Americans give to the winner. It doesn't matter if you're a banker or if you run a gas station . . . you have a chance to win, winning is great, and winners are esteemed and held in envy. My gosh, there are countries where they shoot the winner. We glorify him . . . and then try to emulate him. Our acceptance of winners . . . I think the Super Bowl is an extension of that.

"And I never felt like we had to slink out of town.''

How would you feel, based upon what's gone before, if the Vikings went back to the Super Bowl?

"I don't think I'd feel any differently. I hope I'm enough of a realist to know what's got to happen in order for us to win. If we prepare well and if we then go out and execute, the chance of winning is great.''

And the reality of dealing with losing the Super Bowl?

"You have to come down,'' he said. "You've been going for an entire season, up on a level sustained by emotion and activity. All of a sudden, it comes to a stop.

"There are coaches who can't wait to get back and look at the film . . . to keep themselves immersed in football. That's not my way.

"The first thing I have to do is suffer some. That line about show me a good loser, and I'll show you a loser . . . I think it has a lot of truth to it. That's the reason we discourage players from standing on the field after a game to visit with people from the other team. I don't believe you can play a football game, where people are beating on each other for three hours, and suddenly turn off some switch and stand around and smile and visit. There's a time for that, fine . . . but it's after you've had a shower and dressed. It isn't a switch you can throw the minute the game ends.

"That's the reason I don't seek the other coach out to shake hands after a game. I'll never embarrass him . . . I wouldn't refuse to shake . . . but I'll never make the first step.''

What did Grant do after the Super Bowl losses?

"Got out of the routine for a few days. I spent time at home . . . I enjoy just being at home.''

Has he ever attended a Super Bowl game he didn't coach in?

"No."

Has he watched all of them?

"Not all . . . I've been pheasant hunting a few times on Super Sunday. I'm not much of a one for watching somebody else's football game on television . . . if I painted houses for a living, I wouldn't want to paint the kitchen on the weekend."

What does Bud Grant think of the Super Bowl?

"I think the name is perfect, it is super. It's good for people, it's good for the country . . . it's stimulating, and it serves a real purpose because it gives a great gathering of people something to focus on and have as a common interest.

"It's a colossal, from the standpoint of spectacle . . . I suppose you could accomplish the same thing if you took the best rock bands and had all of them on a stage in the Coliseum. It is that level of entertainment and competition. All of the events surrounding the game help make it super . . . it's an honor to have been a part of it."

And in closing?

"You can work like a dog in preparation . . . seek every bit and scrap of advantage and edge that you can. That's really all you can do. But it doesn't always come out the way you'd want."

And do you ever wonder why?

"No," said Grant. "There are some things you have to accept."

10

Pat

In February of 1947, University of Minnesota coed Pat Nelson walked through the Student Union and got her temper up in the process.

"I saw Bud coming toward me," she said, "and my blood started boiling. I stuck my nose up in the air and started to sail past him . . . the last thing I was going to do was speak to him."

But she did.

Bud Grant caught her arm.

"Don't you speak to acquaintances?" he asked.

"Not to you," Pat Nelson replied. "He asked me what was the matter," she recalled. "I said, 'You have got the nerve to ask me that? You are the rudest person I've ever met in my life!'"

What brought all of this on, as the fellow said, was a failure to communicate.

In the fall of 1946, Pat Nelson had taken on the assignment of seeking a blind date for a friend. A fellow she knew suggested Bud as candidate.

The problem came when Grant was thrust forward for introduction without having been told why he was being thrust forward. Being the shy sort, he just said hello and left.

Moving back to February of 1947, Grant still didn't know he'd angered Pat Nelson . . . or anybody, for that matter . . . and asked for an explanation. He suggested they sit down and talk.

"I don't know," said Pat, "maybe he was intrigued with me. By then, all the girls on campus knew who he was because he was an athlete and so nice-looking. Here I was, telling him he was rude and that what he'd done was terrible."

Grant asked what the terrible thing was that he had done.

After thirty minutes of conversation, things seemed less terrible.

Bud explained that he hadn't known he was being sized up as a possible date for Pat's friend.

Pat Nelson accepted the explanation and was ready to leave when a reporter from the Minneapolis *Tribune* approached and asked if she and Grant would take part in a survey on favorite songs.

"This is so weird," she recalled, "because if that fellow hadn't happened along just then, I would have gone about my business. But we agreed to do it. Then, he asked us to wait because a photographer was coming, and they needed a picture for the story. It was just a coincidence . . . neither one of us had a class the next hour, so we agreed to wait. Why Bud agreed to do it, I'll never know . . . I didn't think it was unusual at the time, because I didn't know him, but looking back, I know that wasn't like him, at all. We waited almost an hour for that photographer, and that's really what made the difference, because we spent the hour talking, getting acquainted."

Carrying weird a step further, Grant is a poor candidate for a "favorite song" survey. He is tone-deaf. "I know how important the National Anthem is to him," Pat explained, "but he couldn't sing it in tune."

"After we talked," said Pat, "I was still getting over being mad at him, but I suppose I was at least a little interested in him."

Bud called her the following evening, inquiring if she had seen the story and photo in the *Tribune*. He then asked if she would like to attend the Minnesota basketball game that Saturday night.

"I said, 'Well, fine . . . sure.' He said, 'I'll leave two tickets for you, you can bring a friend.' "

Pat hung up puzzled. She wasn't sure just what sort of an invitation had been tendered. She decided it had better mean Grant intended to see her after the game, so she took a girlfriend and waited in the seats following the game.

"After a while," she said, "Bud came wandering up. We walked my girlfriend home, and then he walked me to the streetcar line. Looking back," said Pat, "I'm sure I didn't realize that he wasn't used to dating." But that wisdom wasn't available as Bud escorted her to the trolley line on campus. "I thought to myself, If he puts me on the streetcar and sends me home, that's it," said Pat.

Fate . . . only recently decked out as an inquiring reporter . . . now took the form of an automobile. As Pat and Bud waited for the streetcar, a friend of Pat's and her date drove by and offered them a ride.

"I said, 'Great,' and jumped in," Pat recalled. "Bud kind of hesitated for a minute, but then he got in, too."

It was three years later before Pat learned Grant had no intention of getting on the streetcar to St. Paul with her that night. "I was shocked at first," she said. "If that would have happened, our relationship would have been over before it started. Now, though, we look back and laugh about it.''

It wasn't what you'd call a whirlwind courtship.

They saw each other on Wednesday nights during the school year.

"It wasn't my idea, it was Bud's," said Pat. "We never went out weekends . . . weekends were for games or for fishing or hunting.''

What did they do on Wednesday nights?

"Went to the movies or to the library," she said. "We were both poor.''

Was that the extent of Pat's social life?

"We'd see each other on campus and talk on the telephone a couple of times a week, but I went out with other boys, too. I mean, I would have rotted if I'd sat and waited for him. We didn't go out on a Saturday night until the year before we got married.''

They were the same age, but Pat was a junior when they met, and Bud was a freshman. She had finished high school early, and Grant's college career had been delayed by the year spent in the navy. And for a time, Pat thought Bud was older.

"He showed me an I.D. that said he was twenty-six," she recalled. "He didn't admit it was a fake until that first summer . . . I thought I was dating an older man.''

But only once a week.

If durability is a trait admired by Grant, and it is, then his wife-to-be evidenced it from the outset. She saw less of him in the summer than she did during the school year. Bud went to Wisconsin and spent his summers on Simms Lake, near Gordon. He and Bill Blank, a boyhood chum, had purchased land on the lake when they got out of the service. It is the site of the present Grant summer home, but in those days Bud lived in a tent.

"The Cities were the last place he wanted to be in the summer," she said. "He'd write three or four times during the summer, and he'd come down to visit once or twice, but I didn't see much of him.''

How did Pat Nelson, who was outgoing and social, respond to this absentee ballot form of romance?

"I knew I liked him, and I knew he liked me," she said, "but I thought it was unusual. If Bud would have had such a thing as a girlfriend, I probably would have been the girlfriend, but he has a hard time committing himself. He still does. If I say, 'Can we do this next week?' he'll always leave himself an out. He's cautious in his relationships.

"I didn't realize that at the time," she said, "and I used to get very hurt. I'd think, 'Gee, people think I go with Bud, but he's never around on weekends.' I had to go to parties or dances with somebody else . . . I liked to dance, but Bud doesn't dance.

"I don't think I really had him figured out," she said. "Bud didn't seem like the marrying kind, but almost from the start, he talked about getting married someday. I think we knew we were committed to each other, even though we weren't together a lot."

It wasn't a normal courtship, but then Grant's way never has dovetailed consistently with what the rest of us regard as normal.

"I think Bud was reluctant to fall in love," said his wife. "I don't think he wanted to care that much about someone, because that would put restraints on him. I also think he was lucky to find a girl who was independent, too . . . someone who could keep up a relationship where he was able to be himself.

"We get along well," said Pat Grant, "because I don't always agree with him. Bud respects that. Our ideas are so different about so many things . . . we can argue about politics or a lot of things. He might not agree with me, but he respects my opinions."

Although marriage may have been in the conversation early on, the future didn't really begin to take shape until late in the summer of 1949, before Grant's senior football season at the University of Minnesota. And the elements that fixed the chemistry were a near failure and an assumption.

Bud had received a failing grade in a history course during spring quarter of his junior year. In order to assure his eligibility for the football season, he had to make up the failure. "He's really good in history," said Pat, "but I don't think he liked the instructor."

Bud didn't want to stay on campus for summer school, so he opted to take the makeup course in history by correspondence. He was a strong candidate for All-American honors in 1949, so there was pressure on him to make up the failed course.

But Bud is, his wife noted, a "terrible procrastinator. He kept putting the correspondence lessons off. Finally, toward the end of the summer, he admitted he needed help. I was working, but I had vacation time coming, so I took two weeks off. We spent the two weeks in the library . . . I think there were seventeen of those stupid lessons, but we finally got them done.

"Bud was really grateful for my helping him," said Pat. "I think he finally had to admit he needed someone. He still doesn't like having to need people, but I guess that, once he had admitted it to himself, he decided he might as well marry me."

Which was when the assumption came into play.

Pat's career goal was to become a food editor for a newspaper. She had divided her studies at Minnesota between home economics and journalism, and she had a job opportunity in Cleveland.

"I told Bud about it, and he was shocked," she said. "He said, 'Well, aren't we going to get married next year when I get out of school?' I told him that was the first I'd heard about it. He said he just assumed I knew he wanted to marry me. He said, 'I thought you knew that's what our plans were.' "

Pat suggested those were the sort of plans that should be discussed and not assumed.

They were married on August 11, 1950, in a chapel on the University of Minnesota campus.

And with a not-too-normal prelude.

"Bud had two wisdom teeth removed . . . I mean surgery, with a lot of stitches . . . either the day before or two days before we were married," said Pat. "His face was all swollen up. And then, when we were leaving my folks' house for the chapel, the photographer had to tie Bud's tie . . . he didn't know how to do it."

Their honeymoon came later.

"We went duck hunting," Pat Grant advised, with no particular register of warmth to her tone. "We stayed in this awful little hotel in a room right next to the kitchen. It wasn't really even a room . . . the wall between us and the kitchen was a partition that didn't go all the way to the ceiling. The cook started banging pots and pans around at about three o'clock in the morning, getting breakfast ready for the hunters."

Her one (and only) duck-hunting trip included being abandoned in a duck blind while her new husband spent much of the day elsewhere, in pursuit of ducks.

"He wouldn't let me take my radio, we didn't have anything to eat all day long, it rained, and I got chased by a cow," Pat recalled. "And when he went off by himself, he left me with a loaded gun. I could have killed somebody! I guess he trusted my judgment."

Pat's overview on duck hunting?

"I think a lot of what happened happened so that I'd never ask to go duck hunting again."

If truth be told, she had been hunting with Bud once before that.

He took her grouse hunting near the Simms Lake property in Wisconsin before they were married. Pat fired one round from a shotgun, striking a telephone pole. Walking back, on an ancient log road, she twisted her knee so badly that Grant practically had to carry her.

"Those were my two hunting trips," she said.

The newlyweds purchased a small log cabin home on Forest Lake, north of St. Paul. Shortly after they moved in, Bud rejoined the Lakers for basketball training camp.

Pat was working then in St. Paul, but there was this one problem . . . she didn't know how to drive a car. At least, she didn't know how to drive a car very well.

"Bud taught me," she explained. "Bud's idea of teaching was to put me behind the wheel and say, 'Go ahead and drive.' It's a good thing I've had such steady nerves. Anyway, I was driving, hardly knowing what I was doing, but I didn't have a license. Bud said I should go up to Center City and take the test for my license . . . I'd been driving for about two days, I think.

"He said I might not pass the test the first time, but it would be a good experience for me. Well, I went up there, innocently, and I gave that poor driving inspector the ride of his life. When he said, 'Stop,' I put on the brakes so hard the poor guy just flew. I couldn't park . . . I failed that part of the test, too . . . I'd never parked a car in my life. I was just numb.

"I went home and said to Bud, 'Why'd you have me do that?' It was a good experience, all right."

Let the record show that Pat did get her license . . . on the third try.

She was asked how one survives in a marriage where the partner is going to do things his way.

"I save my stubbornness for the big issues," Pat explained. "I let him go his own way until there's a point where something really means a lot to me. Then, I'll say, 'You might not want to do this, but I really want you to do it.' I don't say that very often, but when I do, he usually does what I want."

She said that living with a dominant figure has helped to make her a stronger person.

"You can break, or you can become stronger," said Pat. "There's no sense sitting around feeling sorry for yourself if things don't go your way. And I think Bud respects the fact that I don't let him stomp all over me."

We have the "telephone at the lake" case as evidence of these truths.

For some years, the master of the Simms Lake home near Gordon declared that there would be no telephone. And that was fine until the kids got older, when the lack of a phone became a problem. Pat, for example, thought such things as communicating the birth of a grandchild might be reasonable cause for having a phone installed. Then there was worrying when she knew one of the kids was scheduled to drive up but wasn't sure of arrival times. "I'd be up half the night," she said.

Enough, already.

"Bud," said Pat, "I'm going to get a phone at the lake."

She bought it as a birthday present for Bud, a telephone that looks like a duck . . . and quacks, as opposed to ringing.

"I paid a fortune for the stupid thing," she confessed. And wisely, it turned out . . . while Grant the guardian of privacy still grumped about the prospects of a phone at Simms, Grant the naturalist couldn't help but admire its form.

Pat handled the installation, of course.

With the phone in place, one iron-clad rule was set down: Nobody, but nobody, gets the number. Pat gave the number to one of her brothers with instructions that it was to be used for genuine emergencies only. None of the kids gave it out. Even Sid Hartman, the newsman woven so firmly into the fabric-Grant, doesn't have the number. "I won't give it to him," said Pat. "I'm sure there have been times when he'd like to wring my neck, but I won't do it."

But the phone does ring . . . rather, the phone quacks. And for whom does the duck quack?

"For Bud, of course," said Pat Grant. "Who sits and talks by the hour? Bud! He loves it. He calls his buddies, and they call him. If he's there alone, he calls home every night.

"That is so typical of our relationship," she added. "I fight tooth and toenail to get something, and he ends up thinking it's great."

The Grants have six children, Kathy, Laurie, Pete, Mike, Bruce, and Danny. As of this writing, the girls and Pete are the only ones married. Also, as of this writing, there are six Grant grandchildren.

"Bud wanted our kids to respect him," said Pat. "He was fairly strict with them, but he didn't want them to be scared of him. Now, the grandchildren . . . he isn't stern with them, ever. He's putty in their hands, and it's nice to see.

"Bud has always been a wonderful father," Pat said. "I mean, long before Woman's Lib, he changed the pants and fed the babies, and he liked doing it. He is great with them. People probably wouldn't think it, but Bud is terrific with babies and little kids . . . he loves them. He has a great rapport with all children. When he played, and even after he got into coaching, he was around the kids a lot, and he thoroughly enjoyed it."

He may have been a loving father, but Grant evidenced a lower boredom threshold than did his wife.

"When the boys were in Little League . . . you know, those games where it's 22–0 after two innings . . . Bud usually had something to do that kept him away from the games," said Pat. "But I went . . . I went to all of them."

Perhaps, the suggestion was made, Bud stayed away because he didn't want his presence to put undue pressure on the boys.

Pat Grant cocked an eyebrow.

"When they were on high school teams," she pointed out, "he never missed a game."

And that annoyed her, to a degree.

"Of course, there are a lot of things I do that annoy Bud," she added. "Maybe that's the secret of a good marriage, being able to live with the annoyances."

Pat Grant says her husband may chafe at things boring, but deserves high marks whenever full-blown problems might arise.

"If there is ever a crisis," she said, "Bud is the person I would want there with me. He has that marvelous calm about him."

Pat Grant worked to put herself through college. Her father was, in her words, a "creature of the depression." He owned a hotel and restaurant, lost both, and drove a truck before settling as a machinist. "We didn't have a lot of money," she said.

Which matched her closely with Grant, the son of a Superior, Wisconsin, fireman.

"The first time Bud took me to Superior to visit, his dad met us at the train station with a fire truck," she recalled. "His dad was a wonderful guy . . . a character, really, but a nice man. When we lived in Winnipeg, Bud's folks would come to visit, and by the time his dad had been there a day or two, he'd know more people in the neighborhood than we did. He was that way . . . people just opened up to him."

On one visit to Winnipeg, Bud's father took his daughter-in-law aside and expressed his concern on a subject that had been troubling him. Kathy and Laurie were toddlers at the time, and Pat was pregnant with Pete.

"He said Bud was at a critical stage in his career and that he shouldn't have the worries of a big family along with the responsibilities of his job. He told me," Pat added, "that I shouldn't be having so many kids."

Her response?

"I told him he was talking to the wrong person."

The Grants live on a lake, some five minutes from the Vikings offices in Eden Prairie.

Do they have drop-in neighbors?

"Not really," said Pat. "Bud's the type you would let know before you dropped in . . . he values his privacy so.

"But he is very fond of an older lady who used to live next door to us, Mary Martin. Mary dropped in. She and Bud had this absolutely great relationship. That's Bud, again . . . he's good with older people, too."

She smiled.

"Kids, older people, dogs, and fellows he likes to hunt or fish with . . . he trusts them."

The smile widened.

"But he doesn't understand women! After all these years, he doesn't understand women."

While there is no context for this next bit, we go back in time to set straight a story told in error, down the years, by this writer.

It was 1969, and the Vikings were to play the Los Angeles Rams on the Coast, late in the year, in a game of significance. The Rams had won eleven in a row, and the Vikings had won ten straight.

I was the Viking PR man at the time, and I was in Los Angeles early in the week, advancing the game. One segment of my assignment took me to a midweek broadcast luncheon, where I ended up seated at the head table next to George Allen, then the head coach of the Rams.

Somewhere between the salad and the broiled chicken, George asked if I had spoken to Bud recently.

I told him I had tried the previous night, but hadn't reached him.

George nodded and smiled that flinty little smile of his. His tone was conspiratorial. "At the office, studying films, probably," George suggested.

I'd been afraid he was going to say something like that.

I reached for a roll. "To tell you the truth," I replied, "he was hanging wallpaper in the downstairs bathroom. Pat said she didn't want to interrupt him."

George pushed his chicken aside and sat in stony silence until it was his turn at the lectern.

And the Vikings whipped the Rams pretty handily on that Sunday.

Now, after all these years, George, I find out he wasn't hanging wallpaper in that downstairs bathroom . . . he was putting up a new mirror.

"It had to be the mirror," Pat assured me. "We only wallpapered once together, and that was at Forest Lake. It was the closest we ever came to a divorce. The time you're talking about, Peter and his friend were trying to put up this big mirror, but they dropped it and chipped a corner. Bud saw that and decided he had better take care of putting up the mirror. But he tightened the screws too much and cracked it. I ended up buying two mirrors."

These two are opposites, the Grants, yet their differences meld in a solid union, which is another way of saying they are well-married. They play off one another most efficiently. Pat Grant delights in new vistas, in reaching out, and in savoring life from silliness through sadness. Bud lives within a more tightly drawn arc, remarkably self-sufficient and more comfortable with vistas that are familiar and of his own design. Their common bond is their family.

"It's hard to explain our relationship," said Pat, "but from the first time I ever sat down and talked to Bud, I have felt perfectly comfortable with him. I never paid any attention to the 'different' side of him, the way he can be so intimidating. I guess I was just going along my merry way, figuring he was like everybody else."

Two theories were advanced to Pat Grant concerning her husband.

Theory Number One held that Bud is really not a mysterious and complex sort, as so many Grant watchers would have you believe.

Indeed, the theory went, he is a simple person, and he keeps his life and his philosophies uncluttered and direct.

Pat Grant agreed. "He loves that," she said, referring to the reserve many people feel obliged to evidence around Grant. "It reinforces the distance he's able to keep between himself and those people. The book *The Art of Intimidation* . . . Bud could have written it."

Curiously, he gives the appearance of being more approachable to the public, to the fan.

"He really is good with people when he's out in public," Pat pointed out. "If someone comes up to talk or to ask for an autograph, he's never impolite. And sometimes, it can be hard. We were at a place downtown with some friends from Winnipeg, and Bud could hardly eat his dinner for the people who kept coming over to our table. And they were nice people, I don't mean to sound stuck-up or anything like that . . . they meant their actions in the nicest possible way. It's a tribute to him, really, and he realizes that. But it's still hard to eat."

Theory Number Two was advanced: Her husband is selfish. Or, at the very least, he has strong self-awareness.

"I know what you mean," she said. I've told him that, too, lots of times." She paused . . . much the same as Bud will . . . making sure the words are going to come out right.

"I think he is constructively selfish," she said. "He's selfish with his time. We've discussed this, and I think he agrees with me."

He's Bud Grant, and he doesn't believe in gingerbread.

As children, most of us are simplistic and then again as oldsters, as our circle swings near to full. In between, though . . . through our "living" years . . . we accept all sorts of roles in the playing out of our lives. It's not necessarily right, mind you . . . or healthy, for that matter . . . it's just accepted. We spend a god-awful amount of time trying to figure out just what it is that others wish us to do or how it is that others wish us to appear.

Watch the child or the oldster. They say, "I want." They don't say, "How would you feel if I . . ." They don't say, "You might not agree with me, but I . . ."

And they say, "I want," without concern as to how their expression will mesh with the wants of others. Great time savers, those children and oldsters, lopping off all the hours and effort the rest of us spend on convention and propriety, to say nothing of the anguish and frustration we purchase so frequently with the same coin.

Bud Grant is as immune to convention and propriety as he is to a keen north wind probing the face of a duck blind.

And not in a mean way.

What was it Pat said? Constructively selfish.

It doesn't always make for smooth sailing, however, signifying nothing more, perhaps, than the fact that the Grants are normally wed.

"What Bud wants to do isn't always what I want," said Pat. "I've gotten used to that over the years, because he's not going to change. That left it up to me to make my peace with our relationship, and I think I've done that. Usually, there is one person in a marriage who is more demanding, and one who is more giving. I don't envy him his way, but we talk our differences out. I know there are parts of my thinking that Bud doesn't understand, just as there are parts of his that I don't understand."

So how does it work?

"Because we love each other," said Pat Grant. "And by keeping a sense of humor . . . that helps, too."

Our conversation was interrupted by the telephone . . . the one at home rings conventionally.

"Oh, hi . . ." was followed by a couple of "umms."

There was a pause, and then Pat said, "We're not going until later on today."

Another pause.

"Your dad and I."

Giggle.

" 'Bye."

She grinned. "That was Kathy . . . she asked me who was going to the lake with me. When I said, 'Your dad and I,' she said, 'Who's he?' "

At the lake, "he" is a different person.

Why?

"Because people there have known him since he was a kid, and they couldn't care less that he's the coach of the Minnesota Vikings. To them, he's just Bud, the guy who has a place over on Simms, the guy who enjoys the same things that are important to them. He loves that. Around here, he's always Bud Grant, the football coach, but over at the lake, he's just Bud Grant. People around Gordon think of him as one of their own."

Why?

"They're very individualistic . . . I think that's why he gets along with them so well. Each one of those people is uniquely himself, yet they have shared interests," said Pat.

"At the lake, people do drop in. We sit and visit, talk about the weather, talk about changes in town, talk about the lake or about the fishing. It's very relaxed. Bud drops in on people, too."

Pat was asked what is the worst thing, for her, about being the wife of the coach.

"The time involved, I suppose," she answered. "He's been coaching . . . my gosh, it's almost thirty years!"

She was shocked when Bud left the playing ranks, at age twenty-nine, to become head coach at Winnipeg.

"I had just assumed he would play four or five more years," she said. "When he took the job, we really didn't know if our future would be in coaching . . . he just had a one-year contract. And Bud didn't know if he would like it or if he'd be any good at it."

Had coaching seemed like a logical step, even if it would have been down the line?

"No. I never thought for a minute that he'd coach. I didn't know what he would do . . . he'd talked some about wanting to have a fishing camp up north . . . but I didn't worry, I knew he'd do something.

"Of course, it turned out that he really did well, and he liked it. Bud likes the manipulation, figuring things out and putting all of the pieces into the right places."

On to more meaningful topics: Is he easy to cook for?

"I've been doing it for so long that I know what he doesn't like . . . he doesn't like creamed things, and he doesn't like macaroni and cheese. I think he doesn't like a lot of the things he had as a kid, because he was from a family that didn't have much, like I was.

"I mean, we had a lot of macaroni and cheese, too, but I still like it.

"Once Bud had a bad experience with something, he's just so rigid about avoiding it," said Pat. "He doesn't like to stand in lines, because he had to stand in line when he was in the service.

"That was forty years ago, for crying out loud! Everybody has to stand in line sometimes."

She smiled. "Everybody except Bud. He didn't get his driver's license renewed for seven years because he didn't want to stand in line."

Following the thread of that episode, we learn the absence of a driver's license was duly noted several years ago by a Wisconsin state trooper, who stopped Bud for exceeding the speed limit en route back to the Twin Cities from their place on Simms Lake. Pat, Danny, and Danny's friend were with him.

The patrolman was young, and upon reaching the car, he obviously recognized Grant. He asked for a driver's license, and Bud handed over his out-of-date papers.

There was a pause, and then the patrolman cleared his throat, and asked if this was the most current license Bud had to offer. Through it all, Grant stared straight ahead, his visage remindful of those faces you can see on Mount Rushmore.

Bud said, Yes, that was the only license he had.

The officer hemmed and hawed a bit, and then noted that the license had been expired "for several years."

"Bud didn't say one word," said Pat. "If it would have been me, I'd have been babbling on about how sorry I was. You talk about intimidation, the poor patrolman was practically apologizing for stopping him.

"He gave Bud a ticket, he had to. We drove on, and no one said a word . . . no one said a word for fifty miles."

Bud had to take the driving test over, in addition to paying his fine.

"He wasn't the least bit upset about it," said Pat. "He got caught, he had to pay seventy-five dollars or whatever the fine was, and he had to take the test over. He probably thought it was a good exchange . . . he'd gone seven years without standing in line."

For some, communication with Bud Grant is no more difficult, say, than trying to pin a hair ribbon on a lightning bolt. He has this built-in time lapse to his responses . . . sort of like if you were to throw a silver dollar into a well and then wait for the splash.

You say whatever it is you have to say, and then you wait.

Bud looks at you. Then, he might tidy up a pile of papers on his desk or resettle himself in his chair. He'll suck a tooth or scratch his head or gaze at something behind you that you can't see. Finally, the words come out . . . in the manner of a merchant measuring valued coins in change.

"That's part of him," Pat Grant laughed. "You have to learn to be patient, like Bud. He forces some people into babbling, because they feel uneasy when nothing is being said."

Why does he do that?

She shrugged. "I don't think he knows why . . . he's always been that way. It isn't that he sets himself up as being superior to other people . . . it isn't that, at all."

Could be, Grant feels answers given thoughtfully . . . communications carried out accurately and clearly . . . are more important than the haste in which a response may be made.

Does Pat Grant communicate with her husband?

"You bet."

More to the point, if something's bugging her, can she tell him about it?

"Right away," she confirmed.

Does he talk to you if something's bugging him?

"Not in the same sense, but things don't bug him."

What about when he gets mad and . . .

"He doesn't get mad. He might get annoyed . . . he doesn't get annoyed with people so much as with what they do."

Does the wife of the coach ever wonder if the fans ever wonder about her?

She laughed. "I don't think so. People think about a coach in the NFL as this overwhelming presence, but I don't think they stop to think about wives or families."

And that suits Pat Grant just fine.

"I made up my mind, a long time ago, that Bud would do his thing, and I would do mine. I am in charge of our home. I enjoy that. It really bugs me when I hear women say it's so boring, being at home and being a mother. It's not boring! You make decisions, you budget your time and your efforts, you take charge, really, of the actions of your kids. To me, it's like holding an executive position in a company."

Still, there is the matter of being Bud Grant's wife in the business of living.

"I don't go out of my way to tell people who I am," she said. "Sometimes, it makes people's attitude change. I've seen clerks in stores be unfriendly, but when it dawns on them who I am, they'll be nice as can be. That bugs me. If they're not going to be nice before they find out who you are, they're not going to be nice afterward, either.

"I try to stay outside the public's identification with Bud," she said.

Actually, Pat Grant doesn't need public awareness . . . she's busy enough in private. As these pages were taking shape, she was wishing she could scrape up $350,000.

For what?

Well, there's this horse farm out by Victoria, west of Chanhassen, Minnesota, and she would dearly love to live there. Since the asking price started out at $650,000, Pat recognizes a bargain when she sees one.

To date, her seeds of suggestion have fallen on meager soil, but she's not giving up.

Bud doesn't like farms, and you can see a cornfield from the bedroom window. Bud also doesn't like horses . . . he got thrown by one when he was a kid.

I, for one, think she'll get the horse farm . . . it's no cinch, but I think she'll pull it off.

After all, she got new carpeting for the living room. We're talking different dollars, here, but that was uphill, too.

"I practically had to give a slide presentation," she said. "I had these lists in my head, all the reasons why the old carpeting should come up, all the reasons why new carpeting would be so much better."

For quite a while, Bud didn't say much more than that he'd think about it.

"Finally, I said, 'Bud, I can't stand that carpeting any longer. I'm going to buy new carpeting!' "

She did, and for all anybody has been able to determine, Bud likes the new carpeting just fine. Of course, he never said so, in so many words.

There you have Pat Grant, the lady who lives next to the Glacier.

She's made some sacrifices.

Rather, she has been willing to change.

You get the feeling Pat Grant would love nothing better than dancing her socks off, and I'll bet she still could. But Bud doesn't dance.

You get the feeling she is a social person at heart and that she would be comfortable going out on the spur of the moment or having friends drop by. But that is not Bud's way.

If truth be told, she has been willing to set aside quite a few of the bells and whistles that were important in the life of young Pat Nelson. But you also get the feeling she believes the trades were well-made.

She has a relationship with her children that most of us can only wish we had . . . parent, mentor, confidante, and friend. Spend a day with her, and you are midstream in a steady flow of Grant children and grandchildren who are comfortable dropping by her comfortable home, even though they don't live there anymore. They pop in, or they phone . . . for advice, to ask a favor, or just to share a bit of laughter.

I wish my kids enjoyed me as much as her kids enjoy her.

She also has an affectionate, durable, and understanding relationship with her husband.

"See, I know him," she pointed out. "I know how he's going to react. Something can happen or something can be said, and we just look at each other across a room, and I know we're thinking the same thing.

"Bud keeps a lot of people at arm's length, but he's never done that with me. When I'm with him, I feel comfortable."

Probably, one of the things Pat Grant didn't do turned out to be one of the most important things she's ever done.

She didn't treat her husband differently than other people.

Good idea.

11

Gordon

"I like being out there.

"I like getting up at five o'clock when it's pitch black. You get into that duck boat, and you have to feel your way out into the slough, because you can't see anything. It smells bad, it's wet, it's cold . . . I like that.

"I suppose writers and poets have been trying, for many years, to explain the attraction. I certainly can't do it any better than they have.

"I think it's a feeling. To watch the sun come up . . . I feel like I'm part of a beginning. You're there when the birds awaken, you hear other creatures. You hear the day coming to life all around you. You hear it, and you can smell it. And then the sun comes up, and you can see it.

"You experience things you could never know unless you're out there."

Bud Grant was not born to play football, nor was he born to coach football. But he believes he was born to be "out there."

"The feeling I'm speaking of, it's not something you can be introduced to," he said.

He is not speaking of the casual fisherman or the social hunter . . . the fellow who's in a bass boat because that's where the client wants to be or on the deer stand because . . . what the hell . . . all the guys are going to be there.

And, for certain, he is not speaking of the hunter or fisherman whose only interest is the killing.

"If it's genuine, I think you're born with it," he said.

Question.

If you love the outdoors and its creatures, do you ever regret killing them?

"No. You hunt . . . and you can hunt a bird or an animal or a fish

141

. . . and it's a challenge. It shouldn't be easy. If you kill, it should be because you want whatever it is you're after.

"A lot of times, when you're duck hunting, the birds are flying too high for a sure shot. You might get lucky and hit one, but chances are, if you do, it will fly on, wounded, to die some place else. I don't make marginal shots. I've been on a marsh and heard guns blazing away when the ducks or geese were too high. Shooting a gun, just being able to blaze away, doesn't do a thing for me. If I want the game and it's within range, I'll shoot it, I'll retrieve it, I'll clean it, and I'll eat it. I'll do all of it . . . not just part of it."

Harry Grant, Sr., accompanied his son on some hunting and fishing trips back around Superior, but it really wasn't his thing.

"It was always somebody else's idea," said Bud. "If a couple fellows from the firehouse were taking their kids fishing, we'd go, too. He went deer hunting with me, because he knew I wanted to go."

Summers, Harry Grant would pack his family into the car and take a week's vacation . . . often down around Gordon, Wisconsin, some fifty miles south of Superior. "We always had old cars," said Bud, "and a limited budget. We didn't go far."

But the trips were the highlights of Bud's young years.

"I hunted," he said. "Looking back, I guess I always hunted."

He made a bow and arrows and stalked sparrows. "If I saw a pigeon, I'd look at in terms of the sort of shot it presented." He had a slingshot, and, when he was of a proper age, a BB gun. He didn't plink tin cans or bottles, though he hunted field mice. He pounded nail holes into the bottom of a coffee can, rigged a pole to it, and hunted minnows.

Come a long way, this mouse stalker . . . he's hunted and fished from the Atlantic to the Pacific and from the Arctic Circle down into Central America.

"I can smell a deer," he volunteered. "I really can. I don't mean every deer, but it's happened. Just as the deer can smell me. They have a distinct odor if you get close to them, from a musk gland in their legs. It's not unpleasant, just sharp . . . if you know it, you know it's deer. That smell is how they keep track of each other, how they know John from George from Joe."

Grant would rather hunt, not stand.

"Something like 90 percent of the deer taken are shot from stands . . . the shooter is up in a tree or in some kind of concealment.

"That's deer standing, not deer hunting.

"Hunting is made up of the things I'm more interested in . . . moving from the panorama of one view to another, bellying up to the top of a rise to get that careful look down into a draw. It's being conscious of wind and sign and cover."

Grant made a wry smile. "I'm not coming out in criticism of people who hunt deer from a stand . . . I'm just saying I feel more on a level with the animal when I hunt it."

Do you stalk ducks . . . or geese?

"You have to move around. You end up in a position, but you have to know why you should end up there. You have to know wind and weather from how they're going to influence the birds. There's a lot more to it than just sitting, waiting, in a blind or a boat. Ducks are fascinating," said Grant. "They follow flight patterns . . . the patterns are invisible to us, but they definitely follow them. The challenge is in getting to the good shot."

He shot a bear once in Canada . . . he has no desire to go after bear again.

"It's more of a shoot than a hunt. Usually, the hunter is in a tree, and the bear is drawn with baits."

Would he be interested in going on safari, to hunt big game in Africa?

"I'd love to see it, but I wouldn't want to hunt it. I have no desire to shoot an elephant, but I'd enjoy seeing the elephant in its habitat. I know a lot of people go on camera safari, taking pictures. I don't think I'd need that . . . I would have enough of a picture in my mind."

He has hunted moose, bear, deer, wolf, and smaller game—coyote, fox, rabbit, and squirrel. He has hunted geese, duck, pheasant, quail, ruffed and sharp-tailed grouse, raven, and crow.

Crows?

"Crows and ravens are the smartest birds that fly," he said. "A duck or a goose will see movement, but a crow or a raven will see you. Big difference. If you stay still, the duck won't distinguish you from the setting you're in. But the crow will and the raven . . . they'll be able to tell that you're something different than the tree you're sitting under. They are extremely observant and wily. They're a scavenger bird, and a scavenger relies on its sight."

More years ago than I care to remember, Grant and I were touring southern Minnesota on a week-long junket, promoting the Vikings during the off-season. We were driving, I think from Rochester to Austin . . . it was late afternoon and a glorious spring day.

We visited as we drove, but I could tell Bud was doing some watching, too. Eventually, he had me turn off the highway, onto a side road. There was a stand of big trees, maybe a hundred yards off the road, on our right. He directed me past the grove of trees, to a farmer's lane, where we could turn around.

Then he had me stop.

"You stay here," Grant said. He got out, opened the back of my station wagon, and rummaged in the young mountain of gear he had stowed there upon our departure from the Twin Cities.

"What the hell are you doing?" I asked.

"Going crow hunting," he murmured, "and don't talk so loud."

He came back alongside my window.

"Don't play the radio, either," he said.

I asked him if breathing would be okay.

"Sure, but don't smoke . . . that'll help your breathing."

With that, the featured speaker from the noon luncheon of the Rochester Rotary headed for the stand of trees. He was still wearing his navy blue sport coat and gray slacks, but he'd replaced his street shoes with hunting boots. He had a .22 rifle in one hand and a crow-calling contraption in the other.

I watched. I've heard people say, kidding, that he can walk over rough country without leaving a trail. He can't . . . but he does have more of a glide than a stride. Then he got into the trees, and I couldn't see him anymore.

I don't know how long he was gone . . . I read the station wagon owner's manual more thoroughly than I have done before or since. And I would have killed . . . or at least maimed . . . for a cigarette.

I never did see a crow. I heard some harsh, raucous sounds, but I didn't know if they were the machine or the real thing. And after a long time, I heard the brief, flat report of the .22 . . . once.

I had finished with the owner's manual and was studying a Wyoming highway map when I saw him coming down the road. He stored his gear, changed shoes, and got back in the car.

"Where's the crow?" I asked.

"I missed."

I managed not to smile, but poorly.

The next morning, we were leaving the motel in Austin for Albert Lea or someplace. I put the brakes on at a stop sign.

Something kind of soft and lumpy dropped onto my braking foot. I'm a decent driver, but not with lumpy things dropping onto my braking foot. I more or less missed the stop sign, reacted to the miss, and then slammed on the brakes in the middle of the intersection. I remember there was a lady in a pickup truck on the other side of the intersection, and she gave me a real queer look.

But I didn't say a word.

After about a block, I looked at Grant . . . he was grinning like a kid who'd just heard that the school burned down.

I gave in when we hit the edge of town.

"Where were you carrying it when you came back to the car?" I asked.

"Under my coat."

"How'd you get it to stay up over the brake?"

"It took a while . . . I got up early."

Bud Grant cherishes hunting, although he is not overly fond of firing guns.

"It's part of it, so I do it, but I'm not a shooter. I know people who will say, 'Boy, did I have a great day . . . I must have burned up a box of shells.' I make no claims to being a crack shot, and I don't shoot trap or skeet."

If he could not carry a gun or a fishing rod, would he still be out in the forests or on the streams and lakes?

"Yes. Hunting and fishing is an excuse to get out there. Bagging a limit doesn't mean much to me. I release most of the fish I catch . . . I only keep what I want for the table.

"Unfortunately, you can't release a bird that you've shot, so I don't shoot them unless I want them."

In recent years, Grant has become increasingly active in wildlife conservation programs. He is the honorary chairman of TIP . . . the initials stand for Turn In Poachers. The program is funded through banquets and the annual sale of wildlife paintings by well-known artists. In one TIP fund-raising project, artist Les Kouba and Grant combined on the painting. He's proud of that. "I'm no artist," he said, "but I really did do part of the painting." So saying, he took down a portrait of a wood duck from his office wall. He pointed to the detail in the wing. "I did that," he said. TIP funds are administered by the Minnesota Department of Natural Resources to obtain information, provide rewards, and aid in the prosecution of poachers.

He is a director of Pheasants Forever, a statewide effort to preserve that handsome game bird. The program deals wth habitat management, winter feeding, and educational programs for farmers aimed at protecting areas of natural cover for the birds.

These aren't "front" jobs . . . Grant works at them. "I have opportunity to be involved in many projects, but I pick my spots," he said. "If I really believe it has merit and it's accomplishing something, I'll get involved."

There have been a lot of years, a lot of time spent "out there." If you are born to hunt and fish, do you ever feel like you're really matching wits with the wild creatures?

"As clever as it may seem, an animal doesn't think. It has instincts . . . some have better instincts than others, that's why they live longer. You learn from them, and you learn something of their ways, but you don't match wits with them. Deer, for example . . . if you hunt deer long enough, you come to learn how they will react. A deer won't go very far on a straight line. You can jump a buck, and he might take off on a line, but within a few yards he'll be veering and cutting. Deer will always work in a circle . . . a lot of animals will . . . coming back across their own trail to learn if anything is following them.''

Grant says he has been at real risk in the bush only once . . . and that time was an occasion of peril and death for many hunters.

The occasion was the Armistice Day blizzard in 1941.

Bud was fourteen years old. Phil Cross, a barber who shared a shop in Superior with Bud's Uncle Jack, had taken Bud and his friend, Bill Blank, duck hunting on Yellow Lake, south of Superior.

"It was very unusual weather," said Grant, "much warmer than you'd expect for November. We rented a little cabin on the lake.''

They hunted in the morning and then returned to the cabin for something to eat. Since only two of them could be accommodated in the duck boat, the two boys went back out to the weedy point where their decoys lay, about half a mile from the cabin. Cross stayed behind.

"We had the boat in the weeds," said Bud. "Bill and I were standing in the muskeg, which is very swampy ground. We had on galoshes, but we weren't even wearing jackets . . . it was a beautiful day.''

For a time.

Abruptly, the breeze from the south fell away, to be replaced by a keen north wind. And it began to snow.

"We were having a grand time," said Grant. "When it started to snow, the ducks just went crazy. We were just kids, excited, and we got a lot of shots." And conditions worsened rapidly.

"It seemed like no time at all, when we couldn't look into the wind any longer," said Grant. "The snow just blinded you. We tried to get the boat away from the shore, but the water was too rough. We realized the only way we could get back to the cabin was to walk back off the point, through the muskeg.''

The ground under their feet was a sponge, broken by potholes of water. And the blizzard roared in on them. "We couldn't walk facing it," said Bud, "we walked backward much of the time." They broke through the surface of the muskeg repeatedly, soaking their feet and legs.

They made it off the point and began crashing through weed beds along the shore.

"I can still remember it so clearly," said Grant. "We were thrashing along, and it dawned on me that we were lost. The wind was so strong by then . . . and the snow was blinding us . . . that we became disoriented. I've heard of that happening to people, and I know it sounds farfetched. But it isn't. And it's very frightening. We had no idea of which direction the cabin was from us.''

But they kept moving. Bill Blank had fallen through the muskeg to where he was soaked to the waist. Both boys wore blue jeans, and now their jeans froze as the temperature dropped.

"We got to where at least we weren't breaking through anymore," said Bud, "and I knew we had to keep trying for higher ground. But Bill lay down in this little crevice, kind of sheltered from the wind, and said he couldn't go any further. I told him we had to . . . I knew we couldn't stay there."

As they argued about going on, the boys heard a train rumbling by, and Bud remembered that there was a train track behind their cabin.

He dragged Bill Blank up a slope, working toward the sound of the train. "We were floundering through the snow, but we found the track," he said.

"Bill said he couldn't go on. He lay down by the track, and I told him I'd find Phil, and we'd be back for him."

Bud followed the railroad track until he found the cabin. Phil Cross was near frantic, but sent Bud into the cabin while he set off to rescue young Blank.

"There was a wood stove in the cabin, but it had gone out," Bud recalled. "I was soaked, and my hands were so numb, I couldn't strike a match. I ended up taking a kerosene lantern and breaking it into the stove. Then I took a wooden match in both hands, dragged it on the metal to light it, and threw it into the stove.

"It practically blew me out the door, but I got a fire started."

Cross returned with Bill Blank, had both boys strip off their sodden clothing, and put them in bed together. He had a half-pint of liquor and mixed it with orange soda pop and had the boys drink it.

Once warmed, the boys dressed in such oddments as were available . . . Bud wore long johns and a pair of waders because he'd only brought one pair of pants. It was still snowing hard and blowing, but they elected to make a run for home.

"We drove and pushed Phil's car up onto the road, and then we started for Superior," said Bud. "We made about twenty miles . . . halfway . . . when we came on three or four cars, stuck on the highway. We couldn't go around them, we couldn't turn back. We were stuck, too. It was drifting bad by then. We spent the night in the car . . . the wind howled all night long. We kept turning the engine on every now and then, trying to stay warm."

By morning, the snow had drifted to near the tops of the cars. All of the stranded motorists met to consider their plight.

They decided Grant was their solution.

"I had on the waders," he said. "They figured I was best dressed to try to find help. I set out and went maybe three or four miles . . . it was still blowing and snowing. I came to a little crossroads store. The man who owned the place was gone . . . he'd been away when the storm hit . . . there was just his wife and two little kids. The power was out, and the phone was out, and the snow just kept coming."

Back on the road, the party Grant had left behind was rescued by a fellow who lived in a cabin off the highway. He took them home with him. "He had just shot a deer," said Bud, "so they had food."

Marooned in the crossroads store, Bud feared that Phil Cross, his friend Bill Blank, and the others had perished. They were equally sure Bud had been lost in his effort to find help.

The blizzard lasted two and a half days. On the morning of the third day, a snowplow broke through from the south, freeing the snowbound cars and opening the road to the store where Bud had holed up.

"We were celebrating being back together when a plow from the north, from Superior, came through," said Grant. "My dad was right behind it, with a fire truck."

There have been other occasions, but Grant attaches less significance to them. Being caught out moose hunting in the Canadian bush, when night fell, and spending the night in a deserted line shack. Once, he was dragging a deer through the woods in a foot of snow when darkness overtook him.

"It's hard enough to walk in the woods when it's dark," he pointed out. "It's very hard when you're dragging a deer." Grant had just made his peace with the notion of spending the night with nature when a pulp truck lumbered past, and its light pointed out the nearby road.

Then, too, there was the helicopter fishing trip in Ontario that led to a twenty-five hour gin rummy game.

Grant and Buzz Kaplan, a fishing pal, were working isolated stretches of Gods River in northeastern Manitoba, trout fishing from a pontoon-equipped helicopter.

"It was great," Bud enthused. "We were fishing places I'm sure no one had ever fished before."

There was a second plane in the party, a prop Cessna, and they kept periodic contact. The return plan was to fly back to the fishing camp at Deer River, but en route, Grant and Kaplan set down for one last cast. The Cessna kept going.

"When we set out again for Deer River, the wind had come up," said Bud. "We discovered we were only making about fifteen miles an hour, flying against the wind. There was no way we'd make Deer River on the fuel we had. Eventually, we set down on an island, about fifty yards long and twenty yards wide . . . a rock, really, in the middle of a big lake. By then it was raining."

The copter's radio, operating on a sight-line basis, was too low to be of much benefit.

"We were there twenty-five hours," said Grant. "We didn't have any food or any wet-weather gear, so we stayed on board. We played gin rummy."

To conserve battery power for starting the copter, they attempted only brief radio messages on the half hour.

At length, one of the signals was heard . . . by a 747 flying at 38,000 feet, bound for Europe.

"We were able to give him a location," said Bud. "He called Winnipeg. The message went from Winnipeg to Barney Lamm's camp on Ball Lake, to Deer River. They brought a plane out from Deer River with gas to get us out."

In the summer of 1946, and fresh out of the navy, Grant and Bill Blank bought sixty acres of lakefront land on Simms Lake near Gordon.

"We were looking for property but not that much," Bud recalled. "The real estate man urged us to buy the whole parcel. I asked him, 'With what?' We only had a hundred bucks each. But the fellow told us we could probably borrow the money if our parents worked and paid their bills on time."

They knew the lake, and they knew the fishing was good, and the price was $1,500 for sixty acres of prime shoreline.

"I went to my dad, very reluctantly," said Bud. "Bill did the same thing." They got the loan and notes of $650 each, to be paid off.

"That bank note was why I scalped football tickets in college," Grant explained.

He had his end paid off after his sophomore year at Minnesota, but then Bill Blank got married and sold his half of the property to Bud.

"So I went back to ticket scalping."

The original parcel has since been expanded to 110 acres, and Grant owns several other sections of wilderness land in the Gordon area. Plans are afoot to build a second lake home.

During those college summers when Pat Nelson saw little of her beau, he could be found in the tent on Simms Lake.

"I had a footlocker for my gear, a sleeping bag, and a good appetite . . . whenever someone from Gordon asked me over for dinner, I was available." He split time, actually . . . he'd hitchhike from the lake, back and fourth to Osceola, to play baseball.

Alone, he fished and learned his lake and land. He got to the point where he even did some guiding for fishing parties.

"It's primarily a bass and panfish lake, but we have walleye," he said. More important, in the rough country off Simms there are trout streams, and Grant is a trout fisherman.

"It's like deer hunting, more of a challenge," he said. "You don't just drive to a dock, get in a boat, and then drive around the lake, trolling a bait. You have to get to the trout stream, that's the big thing . . . and that usually involves going over rough country. When I fish trout, I'm in a stream, wading. You know that when you work your way around a bend, there's going to be a new view. I'm not a purist, I don't tie flies, and I'll fish anything . . . fly, live bait, a spinner. Whatever works. I'm not a big-time fisherman . . . I've fished a lot of places and enjoyed it, but I'm not hung up on having to fish the bone flats or trying for marlin off the Kona coast. A lot of people who do that do it because they think that's what they're supposed to do. I fish because I like it."

The country around Simms is as much a provider as the lake itself.

"There's deer and grouse and duck," said Bud. "I shot my first deer three miles north of the lake when I was fourteen years old . . . I had my Dad's old .32 Remington. I came on a string of nine deer . . . the first eight were does, the last one was a buck. I shot the buck."

When he was fifteen, he shot a ten-point buck near Superior. Harry Grant, Sr., tied the deer to the top of the family car, supposedly to take it on down to the locker plant for dressing and freezing.

"He left it there for three days," said Bud. "I think he showed it to every person in town."

One aspect of Canadian football set especially well with Bud . . . most of the Canadian players worked daytime jobs, so practice was held late in the afternoon. He spent his days, especially when he played, hunting duck and geese on the Delta marshes of Lake Winnipeg and Lake Manitoba.

Just because American football teams practice at more conventional hours didn't mean Grant had to abandon in-season hunting entirely.

Pro teams usually play on Sundays, so they hold a light practice on Saturday morning. Most places, there's a team meeting, and then everybody's on the field by ten-thirty or eleven for an hour of touch-up and fine-tuning. They go through special-team assignments . . . kickoff, kick return, punt, field goal, and so on.

It's a prime opportunity for the network television people to mosey over and visit with players and coaches.

At Minnesota, it was an early mosey.

Grant's teams were on the field by nine and off by ten, and more than once I've seen Pat Summerall walking onto the field just as the players were walking off.

"I'd tell them we were adjusting our body clocks for Sunday, when we'd want to get an early start," Grant reasoned. He was able to say this without smiling, although the players knew better.

Bud would depart Metropolitan Stadium promptly, drive home to collect dogs, gun, and such kids as wished to go along, and then drive an hour north to the Cambridge area to hunt grouse.

"I could get in an afternoon in the field and still get home, clean up, and be at the hotel for the evening meting."

There is also the collecting Bud Grant.

Over the years, the place on Simms and the family home on Bush Lake have seen a steady stream of creatures-in-residence.

Bud's not sure how it began . . . probably with the ravens.

"I was in Wisconsin, and some pulp cutters were taking down a tree that had a nest with two young ravens in it. I said I'd take the ravens."

Ravens look like crows, only a good deal larger.

"A crow will migrate, a raven won't," Grant said. "And ravens are much larger, they can have a five-foot wingspan at maturity.

"I know they don't have reasonng power," he said, "but they come as close to it as any creature I know of. They're almost human, especially in their humor. They like to have fun."

The ravens demonstrated that wit on Bud's dogs and on that durable journalist, Sid Hartman.

"Sid was over at Simms once, and he came out of the house, into the backyard," said Grant. "The ravens liked to sit in this one tree. If you were new . . . if you weren't familiar with the fact that they were there . . . I swear they could sense it.

"Well, Sid walked into the yard, and one of the ravens flapped down out of the tree, hung in the air right behind him, and thumped the back of his head with its feet.

"Sid never came back while we had the ravens."

The dog with the bone was a good deal more long-suffering than Sid.

"The dog would carry a bone out in the yard and get all set to start gnawing on it," said Grant.

"And just like clockwork, the ravens would get after the dog. One of them would get behind him and yank on his tail. He'd whirl around to confront the raven behind him, and the other one would grab the bone and fly up on the roof or into the tree.

"You see a lot of young creatures at play," said Grant, "fox or wolf cubs will tumble around and play. But the raven is the only mature creature I've studied that has a sense of humor. They love to tease. I've seen them devil a fox until the fox just lay down, exhausted. One would nip the fox, and it would whirl around, and then the other would nip. They didn't want to hurt the fox, they were just having fun with it."

The Grants have raised pheasant, duck, quail, ravens, hawks, owls, fox, raccoon, and squirrels.

And Chico.

Chico was a monkey, purchased as a Christmas present for Bud by his wife, Pat.

"I have done some dumb things over the years," said Pat Grant, "but that monkey was the dumbest."

Bud was more charitable.

"The kids bothered it," he explained. "Kids are loud, they move quickly, and they're dashing around. They probably teased it, too."

Pat says Chico was just jealous.

"Danny was little then," she said, "and if he tried to sit on my lap or Bud's, that crazy monkey would nip at his pant legs.

"I got mad at it, and I got a wooden spoon and shook it at him and gave him a good talking-to. I have never gotten a dirty look like that monkey gave me. I no more than set the spoon down when he grabbed it up and started shaking it at Danny, just chattering away."

Chico worshipped Bud, according to Pat.

"He'd go through my pockets at night . . . crawled all over me," said Bud, "to see if I'd brought him a treat."

One of the more durable quotes attributed to Grant goes as follows:

"In order to be successful in this business, a man needs a patient wife, a good dog, and a great quarterback."

He has been blessed with all three elements of that equation, although Tarkenton and Cork aren't with him, any longer.

Of all the creatures he has known, Bud has a special place for his dogs. Cork was a special dog. Grant suffers the occasional house dog his wife visits upon him . . . he raises black Labs.

And the best of a long line was named Cork.

They were together for fifteen years.

Pat says Cork was a one-man dog, and typically Bud doesn't quite agree.

"That's not quite true," he said, "but when I came home at night, he came alive."

You probably don't replace the Corks of life, but Bud's got another good Lab now, Molly. For that matter, he's got a pretty good quarterback, too, in Kramer.

"I've had a lot of dogs," he said. "I keep them if they're smart. If they're not, I give them away. It's like having football players . . . it's easier to win with smart ones."

He's thinking about getting a spaniel, a pheasant dog. "I will," he said, "but not until I leave coaching."

12

A Close, Personal Friend

In Minnesota, it is possible to find members of the sports intelligentsia wearing T-shirts inscribed as follows:

"I'm a close personal friend of Sid Hartman."

This is a role reversal thing, with Sid's readers in a kind of latter-day Chipmunk posture, evidencing all those puckish qualities Merchant and Shrake and that lot brought to their keyboards back in the sixties, when cynicism was no more than a fragile new bud on the greater flower of sports journalism.

Which is another way of saying some of Sid's readers are becoming real smart-asses.

Well, you've got to know Sid to appreciate this. Over the years, I imagine Sid has referenced just about everybody from Pius XII to Willie Nelson by saying, "The guy's a close personal friend of mine."

I guess the T-shirts shouldn't shock me . . . Sid's been saying that for a long time and to a lot of generations.

I can't vouch for the "close personal friend" aspect in many cases, but the thing is, Sid does know everybody. You give Sid a telephone and ten minutes to work it, and he'll have quotes from Tommy La-Sorda, Margaret Thatcher, Dick the Bruiser, and Ted Koppel.

I worked with and for Sid for seven years, and I have known him for thirty years. And I don't know if I'm a close personal friend, but I think I am. I do know this, however . . . for every one thing I've done for Sid, he has done two for me.

Now, the T-shirt aficionados are grinning and giving one another the nudge.

"Yeah," they are saying, "and for every one thing you've done to Sid . . ."

Sorry, fellows, I can't help you. I have groused to and about Hartman . . . often . . . but on the big scores, we've always gotten along.

That's the thing about Sid, the way I see it. If you're his friend, he would do anything for you. If you are not his friend, he can be equally unswerving.

A lot of people think they know Sid, but I wonder.

He's a successful sports columnist and radio commentator who got that way by being a workaholic. He charges just as hard today, when he doesn't have to, as he did when he met Bud Grant for the first time back in 1946. Sid was a part-time sports reporter then; his income came from managing route circulation for the Minneapolis *Times.* He got paid $23 every two weeks.

He is long on energy, short on social graces like small talk and the ability to be, or at least appear to be, relaxed. And he is very tightly wrapped.

Question.

Why would a guy like Bud Grant . . . a rock, secure unto himself . . . become friends for the long haul with a guy like Sid Hartman, who is his total opposite?

And in Grant's eyes, it is a definite and durable friendship. Sid's, too.

Years ago, I came out with a snide reference to Sid in Grant's presence and promptly got about twenty minutes on his feelings for his friend.

I can't quote him, because it was a long time ago, and I wasn't taking notes. But, in essence, he said the following:

A lot of people tease Sid, and that's fine, because he brings much of it on himself. But if someone tries to knock him in my presence, I won't have it. You treat people the way they treat you, not the way somebody else says they treat people. To me, he's been loyal and honest. He's been a friend.

We bicycled the question back to Sid. What base of attraction do you two opposites have?

"We got along from the start," said Hartman, "and I'm not sure why. One thing, I think we've always been able to level with each other. You could see from the start that Bud was his own man. He's a very private person. When he played at the university, the only guys who really knew him were Billy Bye and Jim Malosky. I don't think the other players understood him."

By 1947, when Sid became a full-time sports reporter for the Minneapolis *Star,* he and Grant were friends.

They had dinner together a lot of nights . . . Sid paid and Bud ate.

"We went to a rib joint in Long Lake and to Cafe di Napoli down on Hennepin Avenue. There was this one waitress at di Napoli . . . she'd feed Bud three spaghetti dinners for the price of one. I picked up the check then . . . what was I supposed to do? He didn't have any money. But I'll tell you . . . he never forgot. It's been a lot of years since I've picked up the check when we're together."

Friendship and spaghetti notwithstanding, Hartman still qualified as a cherished target for Grant's most-cherished pastime, practical jokes.

"I had a Buick convertible . . . I think Grant was a senior at the university then," Sid recalled. "I was so proud of that car."

Until it started to smell bad.

"I mean, it smelled awful," said Hartman. "I had the car checked, nothing . . . nobody could figure out why it smelled so bad. I was with Grant one time, and I said, 'What's wrong with this car? What makes it smell so bad?' He looked at me with that poker-face look of his and said, 'If something's wrong, it's something wrong with you, not the car . . . I can't smell anything.' "

However, it wasn't long after that that Bud made sure Sid found the dead crow he'd hidden in the boot where the convertible top stores itself.

They drove to Superior once for New Year's. Sid drove.

"We're on this icy road, I'm really concentrating on the driving, when, all of a sudden, I feel something crawl on my shoe and then start up my pants leg. I almost got us killed. It was a squirrel . . . he'd hidden it in the glove compartment and got it out when I wasn't looking.

"That same trip," said Hartman, "we were on the way back to Minneapolis, and I got a flat tire. It had to be four o'clock in the morning, and we're out in the middle of nowhere.

"I got out of the car, took one step, and fell flat on my face in the snow. When I finally get up and get back to the trunk, there's no spare. I'm snow from head to foot . . . freezing . . . there's no spare, and we're out in the middle of nowhere. I've never seen Grant laugh that hard.

"I told him he was nuts. He said, 'Don't worry, somebody will help us.' And somebody did."

Hartman on Grant's summer baseball adventures: "He'd pitch for one team in the afternoon and another team that night. He wasn't a great pitcher, but he was smart . . . kind of a Frank Tanana of the forties."

On Grant the collegian: "Bud wasn't the greatest student . . . he probably could have been, but he didn't take it that seriously. But he had great street-sense . . . common sense. He was the only player Bernie Bierman permitted to talk in the huddle. I've never made a major decision in my life without talking to Bud first."

On Grant the coach: "I thought coaching was the last thing he'd ever do."

On Bud's departure from, and return to, the Vikings: "I don't think he ever told anyone the full story of why he left. I know that when he did leave, Mike Lynn pulled out all the stops to win with

Steckel, who was Lynn's man for the job. Then, when everything fell apart, it was obvious that there was only one man who could stop the Vikings slide, and that was Grant. So Lynn had to go back to Grant."

How does Hartman feel about Grant?

"I respect him. I respect him because he hasn't changed . . . he's the same guy he was the day I met him at Cooke Hall."

Have they ever had differences?

"Sure, you're bound to. Once, I quoted him about a player in a critical way. He really jumped me. He said he might tell me something in private, but he would never criticize a player publicly. I learned a good lesson.

"I've taken a lot of heat, because of our friendship," said Hartman. "People will say I've got an inside track with him, but in many ways, I have a tougher relationship, because we are friends, than other reporters. In some ways, I'm too close to him.

"But it works, because we both know what our jobs are."

When Grant and Lynn flew to Honolulu to advise Max Winter of Bud's decision to resign, Hartman was with them.

"I'd always told him, 'Sid, when I'm going to quit, you'll be the first to know,' " said Grant. "But I told him he had to fly out to California with us."

When the plane put down on a stopover in Los Angeles, Grant admitted that they were flying on to Hawaii. Sid had the story by then.

And a problem, according to Bud.

"Sid doesn't like to fly over water," he said. "He ended up getting off the plane and flying back to Minneapolis while we went on to Hawaii. He had to sit on the story for twenty-four hours . . . and it was killing him."

Hartman's version is a little less dramatic, but he did admit to being "not too comfortable" with oceanic flights.

Hartman, on the Family Grant: "Pat and Bud are opposites, but they make it work. Bud doesn't say anything, and if Pat had invented the atom bomb, the secret never would have kept. He's good with his kids. I'm more aware of the boys, I suppose, but he's really honest with them."

A few years back, the Grant family threw a surprise party for Sid. Every one of the kids had a gift for him.

Helped, no doubt, to make up for those times like when the raven kicked him in the back of the head.

"That's another thing," said Sid. "He used to insist I go hunting or fishing with him, but he'd also insist that we take just one car. I finally figured it out. We took one car so that when I was frozen or wet or starving hungry, I couldn't do anything about it. He'd tell me it was good for me."

He probably meant it, Sidney . . . he's a close personal friend.

13

Grant On...

The subject was people who had made a lasting impression on him.

"Luther Pettis," said Grant, without hesitation.

The first time Bud ever laid eyes on him was a fine spring Saturday morning when Pettis woke him up in the Phi Delt house on the Minnesota campus.

"I hear you play baseball," said Pettis.

Grant said he did.

"We could use a pitcher at Osceola," came the reply. It was the beginning of a relationship that has endured.

"You meet a few amazing people in your lifetime, provided you're lucky," said Grant. "Lute is one of those people. He had been a farmer, and then went to blacksmithing just when blacksmithing went out of style. He ended up as an engineer with no formal training. He could fix anything . . . with or without tools."

Pettis was construction manager and consultant for a cannery, but that was just a base.

"He had a weekly radio show in Stillwater [Minnesota]," said Grant. "He interviewed people who lived along the river. What he did, really, was tell the story of the river . . . made it come to life . . . through its people. Not everyone can ask questions that make a subject open up, but Lute did that. He put more into that little half-hour radio show of his than most interviewers could have done in a week."

Pettis managed and promoted Osceola's town baseball team. Grant pitched and got paid fifty dollars a game. If he didn't pitch, but played another position, he got nothing. "Lute knew more about people than he did about baseball," said Bud.

"He repaired bikes for every kid in town, and he'd have a story or a riddle or a trick for the kid while he was making the repairs. Nobody picks up hitchhikers anymore, right? Hitchhiking used to be an honest way to travel, but people are cautious now. Lute still picks them up. And he'll buy their lunch and learn their life story, because he's interested in people."

Bud had an old school bell at the place on Simms Lake, and he'd always wanted to hang it but never could figure out how to do it. It was just too heavy and unwieldy. Lute Pettis figured it out one afternoon. Using a couple of ropes and boards, the two of them put the bell up in a cradle.

"We still keep contact," said Grant. "He has season tickets and comes to all the games. I'm comfortable with him. To me, he's a genuine example of what a person can achieve in life, even though he might not have wealth or a formal education."

Grant, on folks you are more apt to have heard of:

Tom Landry, coach of the Dallas Cowboys.

"We've shared a common thread . . . doing what we wanted to do and being where we wanted to be. And we've both been blessed with stable organizations. Tom's met the challenge of living with success on the field. Once the game starts, he's totally involved. He's not a spectator."

Max Winter, owner of the Vikings.

"His greatest quality and his bond is that he has been involved in sport all his life. He has played and coached and managed. It's unusual to have an owner with his background. Max understands . . . he knows there aren't any quick fixes. He has the confidence and the patience to go along with you."

Hank Stram, former Kansas City and New Orleans coach.

"Hank would have made a great crook . . . he'd rather trick you than beat you. He's a good guy . . . it's just that he has so many angles and images that sometimes I think even he must get confused by them. But when we acquired Chuck Muncie, Chuck told me Hank called him right after the deal was made. Hank drafted Chuck at New Orleans. Hank told him Minnesota was a great opportunity for him and that he would be with a good organization and good people. He didn't have to do that, but I appreciated it."

Mike Lynn, Vikings general manager.

"He's not impatient. He'll negotiate with an agent all day long. He never, never interfered with my job. Mike has never so much as hinted at suggesting that I do this or do that. He stays away from the team . . . he never goes to training camp. He is knowledgeable, and he works hard at his job."

Don Shula, coach of the Miami Dolphins.

"He is as committed and intense and as involved in every aspect of football as anybody in our business. It's his life. I don't know what he does for recreation."

Jim Finks, former Vikings general manager who brought Grant down from Canada.

"We had a very good relationship. One of the problems in this business is ego. Jim didn't need a boost all the time . . . he didn't need somebody to tell him he was doing a good job."

John Madden, former coach of the Raiders.

"What you see in those television commercials . . . John's not acting, that's him. I didn't know him well, but he was very involved as a coach. I've been around him when we were out, but John was still talking football. He'd get excited, and those arms would start flailing. I can get too much football, sometimes I'd rather talk about something else. Eventually, I guess he got too much football, too."

Chuck Noll, coach of the Pittsburgh Steelers.

"He's done the best job of coaching I'm aware of. I have tremendous respect for him. To take that team with its different personalities and to hold it on course to win four Super Bowls was a remarkable accomplishment. The ironic thing, to me, is that Chuck doesn't get the credit he deserves when people talk about the great coaches. But that's the way he wants it, I suppose. He doesn't need attention . . . he doesn't want it. I think the example Chuck set . . . not worrying about how much attention he was getting and concentrating on the challenge . . . was what permitted the Steelers to win."

14

Eskimos, Sweat Pants, and So Forth

The man is many-sided.

It was very quiet in the locker room after that first Super Bowl loss against Kansas City. There was just the distant hum of the heating system and every now and then a deep-throated grunt of pain or a curse from Joe Kapp as the doctor worked on his shoulder.

"Goddamned redwood trees," Kapp kept repeating, his face contorted. "They kept fallin' on me, they were like goddamned redwood trees!"

Bud Grant stood in the center of the room, his face as hard and cold as Vatican marble. He was waiting for their fury to subside to where they'd listen.

When he spoke, his voice wasn't loud, but it filled the room.

"I know what you're thinking . . . if only we could play them again, we could do better."

His eyes swept the dirty, shattered faces.

"Well, we can't. It might be different next time, but we just had this time. All we can do is learn from it." His voice took on a cutting edge. "We will learn from it," he said. "We will be a better team for what happened here today."

They opened the season against Kansas City the next year . . . and beat them 27–10. At the team meeting the night before the game, Grant walked in and turned on the Chiefs' Super Bowl highlight film. It didn't have much to say about the Vikings that was good. When the film was over, Bud just got up and walked out.

The Vikings played out of doors until 1981. How cold did it get at the Met?

Following a December win over Chicago . . . the Bears bowed to conditions by enhancing the halftime bouillon with a pint of brandy . . . defensive end Carl Eller faced a band of reporters.

161

"I knew I wasn't cold," said Eller, "because Bud told me I wasn't." He stared down at his large feet then and shook his head wistfully. "But I sure wish someone would have told my feet!"

Grant puts cold weather and its influence on the same shelf with death, taxes, and officiating . . . fates over which the individual holds no sway.

"What can happen is that you don't know what's going to happen," Grant explained in good Casey Stengelese.

"If the cold weather was an advantage for us, it was because we didn't want our players to be concerned about it. We couldn't do anything about it, so why waste time worrying?"

Must have worked . . . the Vikings, from 1967 through 1981, played twenty-five games at the Met after December 1. They won nineteen of them.

Visiting teams mushed into the Met in the manner of Arctic expeditions, done up in thermal underwear, electric socks, and mittens that reached almost to their ears. The Vikings greeted the change of seasons with shirtsleeves, equanimity, and the warmth of Grant's annual storytelling.

He told two stories every year, one about a dog and the other about Eskimos.

"I told the dog story because it had to do with practicing outside in cold weather," Grant explained. "A game's one thing, but practice isn't nearly as attractive. I told them we were like a dog when we went out to practice in bad weather. As it gets colder, a dog's coat grows longer . . . I told them, by going outside, regardless of the weather, our skin would grow thicker and our tolerance for the cold would increase. If we didn't do anything else, we'd get outside for a while."

Grant still enjoyed telling the stories, and claims the teams enjoyed hearing them. "Veterans would tell the new fellows, 'With the weather getting colder, he'll tell the Eskimo story pretty soon.' "

And what was the Eskimo story?

"After World War II," said Grant, "our country built a radar network across the Arctic because there was concern about the Russians attacking us. It was called the DEW line.

"Because of the permafrost, the ground never really thaws out up there, so putting in those big radar installations was a hard job, and it required heavy equipment. The army guys assigned to run the bulldozers would bundle up in all the clothing they could find in order to stay warm. But regardless of what they wore, they could only sit up on those bulldozers for thirty minutes at a time, and then they had to get down and go warm up. As a result, the job fell behind schedule.

"There were Eskimos around the work site," said Grant, "so eventually the army people taught a couple of the Eskimos how to run a bulldozer. The Eskimo would get up on the bulldozer and sit there all day. Before long, they had the job back on schedule.

"The army couldn't figure out why the Eskimo could work in the Arctic while our soldiers couldn't. So they brought the Eskimos down to the States and put them through all sorts of tests. They measured body fat and blood chemistry and hair . . . everything they could think of. They spent half a million dollars on the project.

"And they came up with one conclusion.

"The Eskimo got up on the bulldozer, and he knew he was going to be cold, but he still could run the bulldozer. The army guy got up there and wanted to be warm while he ran the bulldozer . . . as soon as he got cold, he had to get down.

"The moral of the story, as it applied to our team, was that we might be cold, but we could still play football."

There are students of Bud Grant who will tell you that his finest prank may well have been removing all of the commode lids in the Viking office restrooms one April Fool's Day.

There was another, involving a pair of sweatpants, when Grant had the tables turned on him and still won out.

One April Fool's Day his wife, Pat, decided to beat her husband to the punch. He never misses an April Fool's.

Pat got up at the crack of dawn, bundled up the kids, took every last pair of pants Bud owned, and went to a friend's house to hide out.

Grant was to speak at noon at a downtown civic luncheon.

Bud got up when the alarm went off, showered, and surveyed his looted closet. Then he got dressed, had breakfast, and went to work.

Pat called the office right after nine.

"What's he wearing?" she demanded.

"A sport coat, shirt and tie, and sweatpants," came the reply.

She called again, a little after eleven.

"What's he doing?" she asked.

"Getting ready to go downtown, he's speaking at a luncheon."

"And he's still wearing sweatpants?" she wailed.

"Sure . . . he said they're the only pants he's got. But he doesn't seem upset about it."

Pat roared into the parking lot a few minutes later with a pair of pants.

He's part Indian, but he laughs at suggestions of blood having anything to do with his love for the outdoors.

"My dad wasn't an outdoorsman," he points out. He is of French, Scottish, and Indian descent. "My uncle used to tell me I was the only blue-eyed Indian in Wisconsin."

Pro football officiating does not bring out Grant's best side. He is troubled by the fact that games and seasons and careers are influenced mightily by the decisions of men who are not as wholly immersed in the sport as are its players and coaches. Unlike baseball, professional football officials don't work full-time, but leave their regular jobs as salesmen and school administrators and real estate appraisers and so forth to officiate on weekends.

When the Vikings acquired a player from another team, or hired a new coach, Grant debriefed the acquisition and did it with enthusiasm.

"I'm interested," he said. "Another team might have a technique or a training camp drill or a philosophy . . . some aspect of their operation . . . that is better than the way we do a thing. If you take the time, you can learn a lot from new people. It might just be what they eat or when they eat. It helps . . . if nothing new is coming in, you can get inbred."

He will take the time to draw out a shy youngster, but he can be calculatingly cold to a star type.

In 1967, we had Grant and his coaches over for dinner . . . their families had not yet moved to Minnesota.

Pete, our oldest son, was just a toddler then and quite shy.

What with barbecuing out in the backyard and visiting with assistant coaches, I forgot all about Grant. I went inside to look for him . . . he was on the porch, seated, with his back to me. I thought at first glance he'd dozed off because he had his head down. But when I got closer, I saw Pete, sitting in front of Bud, on the floor. They were having a talk. Kids know . . . they can pick out the adults who will talk with them, as opposed to the adults who only talk at them. Pete was smiling and chattering away . . . he'd forgotten all about being shy.

Maybe, he's just an imposing presence to all of us normal, hung up adults.

On a Sunday night, in the old Cadillac hotel in Detroit, he stood in the lobby, waiting for Frank Gifford, who had called to request an interview. The Vikings would play the Lions the next night in a game televised by ABC TV.

As Bud stood waiting, the most-identifiable voice of Monday Night Football rang out across the lobby:

"Harry Peter Grant . . ."

There was quite a bit more, but it was a long time ago. Howard
Cosell kept talking as he walked, and he walked right up to Grant.
There were a lot of people in the lobby, they recognized Howard, and
Howard recognized the fact that he was being recognized. He exe-
cuted one of those wind-depleting, wonderfully complex yet gram-
matically perfect sentences that seem to last for two or three
minutes. You had to admire Howard's lung capacity, especially in
view of the fact that he was a steady smoker.

He ended up his sentence with something like ". . . and what do
you say to that, Coach Bud Grant?"

Gifford was approaching by then, looking vaguely uneasy.

What Bud said was nothing . . . for what seemed like about six
weeks. He stared at Cosell. After a while, Howard's smile took on a
quality to suggest it had been painted into place. Bud just stood
there, staring . . . silent.

Finally, he made a tiny nod and said, "Howard."

Then he turned to Gifford and said, "Let's go up to my room,
where we can talk."

It was, at least to one witness, a devastating thing to do . . .
Howard was left in their wake, cigar drooping.

The thing is, Grant doesn't appreciate people who trundle their
own spotlight around with them.

He is comfortable around people he knows . . . although the re-
verse of that theory isn't always true.

He had all the Viking staff members and their wives over to his
house for dinner the night before a training camp. It was the cocktail
hour, before the lake trout dinner, and Bud was being the perfect
host. There were ice-cold Leinenkugels from the basement bar, and
everyone was having a good time.

My wife was seated on a couch, visiting with Susan Patera, whose
husband Jack was the defensive line coach. Neither one of those
ladies is a conversational slouch . . . they started out lamenting a
mouse discovered in one of their basements and promptly expanded
the topic to spell out, quite clearly, their mutual discomfort with wild
creatures in general.

Grant stood behind the bar, watching and listening. After a time,
he just sort of ambled away, presumably for more Leinenkugel,
which is a Chippewa Falls, Wisconsin, beer and Bud's favorite. Bud's
not really a beer authority, but it is good.

He returned, but not with more Leinenkugel . . . what he had was
a fat, full-grown raccoon tucked under his arm. The ladies were still
visiting at a gallop, so Grant just eased the raccoon down on the edge
of the couch, right behind my wife. The ladies didn't notice at first,

and the raccoon just sat there, looking sleepy. But it must have moved against her, because my wife turned and saw it.

She's got a good yell under normal conditions, but this one was special. Both ladies more or less jumped into each other's laps.

Grant, behind the bar again by then, looked surprised. "I thought you knew we had a pet raccoon," he said.

Part of being the coach is dealing with the media. Is it a hard part?

"I can't say that it is," said Grant. "It's an important part of the job, and it's also a tool. You either take the time, or you take the consequences. I prefer to take the time. Some writers don't want to hear what you have to say, because it might not jibe with what they want to write. But it's important to take the time, to keep the record clean, and to be in a position where the reporters will come to you with their questions."

Grant ignores articles or reports that are either inaccurate or caustic.

You mean, if someone writes a piece and takes a strip off you, you ignore it?

"That's what I mean."

Will you still talk to that reporter?

"Sure, and I hope he wouldn't be able to notice any reaction on my part to what he wrote or said."

What would be wrong with saying you thought the piece was unfair?

"It would be wrong," Grant said, "because then I would have to enter into a dialogue over it, and I would prefer just to ignore it."

What if someone writes a piece that you like?

"I'll let him know," Grant answered.

Football seasons, like new trousers, seem awfully long. Instant reaction . . . elation over a win, despair over a loss . . . can prompt a very dangerous fatigue. The coaches who seem to prosper are those who view the season in long form, realizing there will be ups and downs, rather than give in to those jarring, weekly vignettes of emotion.

"There is an advantage," said Grant, "to having coached for a long period of time. I would imagine that Bill Walsh, for example, finds it easier to coach now than he did early on. I think you become more comfortable with yourself . . . you come to know yourself, really, your strengths and your limitations. And you realize the emotions you are feeling aren't any different from those someone else is experiencing. You learn that you don't have all the answers . . . you still look for them, but you admit to yourself that you're never going to have all of them."

Bart Starr, the former Green Bay coach, asked a question of Grant a few years back.

"He asked if we had a secret for coming back," said Bud. "He wanted to know how we could look so bad one week and then bounce back, and play well the next. Bart said he thought our trademark was that we didn't stay bad . . . we might play poorly one week, but we'd bounce back. He wanted to know what we did that was different.

"The only answer I could come up with was that we didn't do anything different," said Grant, "whether we won big or lost big. Maybe that's the answer."

He was not a "method" or "system" oriented coach. He was no more bound to one philosophy of football than he would be to one hunting tactic . . . he took advantage of cover and terrain in both.

His early Viking teams were strongest on defense, because that's where the team's best athletes were. Yet, they weren't all great athletes. Page certainly and Eller and Marshall were up front, and their rush was a thing of fury. But the secondary was modest in ability. The thing the secondary did was play with discipline. The hinge between the two groups was that free-booting corp of linebackers, Winston, Warwick, and Hilgenberg. The mesh of the entire unit was marvelous.

Yet, when Tarkenton came back, the emphasis went to offense because the circle had run on . . . the better athletes were on offense. Tarkenton, and later Kramer, gave Grant and Burns full range of offensive motion . . . and receivers like Gilliam and Rashad and Sammy White and Foreman made a sophisticated passing attack a necessity, rather than a luxury.

He once had the mayor of Winnipeg don a Blue Bomber uniform and, unannounced, run the opening kickoff back in an intrasquad game. "We had it blocked beautifully," said Grant, "but he ran out of gas at the 20 and fell down."

He has been criticized for his low-key approach to the challenge of preparing players emotionally for a game. He ignores the criticism.

"They're professionals, and this is their job," said Grant. "It's up to each man to prepare himself . . . I can't do that for him. We don't pretend that what we do is the best way," said Grant, "but we try to deal in facts. We try to look at people and situations as they really are."

His normal office uniform during the season is a flannel shirt, corduroy trousers, and scuffed moccasins. If he must wear a tie, he wears a clip-on.

* * *

The times have changed. Nowadays, athletes have joined their peers within the entertainment industry as millionaires.

Can a million-dollar halfback still get down . . . grab grass and growl . . . when the need arises?

"There is no easy solution," said Grant. "Just because a team pays the most money doesn't give it a guarantee on winning. You placate people with money, but you don't buy them unless they are willing to join the effort. It's hard to buy winning."

15

A Most Enjoyable Year

Bud Grant would assess the 1985 Viking season at four o'clock on a winter's afternoon.

"I can't do it any earlier," he explained. "I promised Kathy [his eldest daughter] I'd go with her to look at a house they're considering."

The season, like Sunday brunch at your town's best hotel, had something for everyone.

Excitement.

The Vikings were competitive once more . . . no juggernaut, to be sure, but competitive. They won seven games and lost nine, but five of the losses were by seven points or less.

They were, literally, inches short of winning at Anaheim against the Rams and at Milwaukee against the Packers. Two wins there, instead of two losses, would have put them into the playoffs. At Philadelphia in December, they trailed 23–0 with 8 minutes remaining to be played.

They won the game, 28–23, certainly sealing the fate of embattled Eagles coach Marion Campbell, once a member of the Vikings coaching staff.

There was controversy.

The dispute over control of the franchise spilled out of the board room and onto the pages of newspapers across the country. The local media, for its part, sparred with Grant over access to the team's locker room. And that contretemps followed on the heels of Bud's skirmish with ABC-TV on the issue of televising the National Anthem.

And, finally, there was final shock. . . .

Grant resigned.

Again.

All of this made for an enjoyable year?

"As enjoyable a year as I can remember," Grant affirmed.

"We had more new people than we'd ever had before . . . new players and new coaches, young people. I found that very stimulating.

"Our games were suspenseful," said Grant. "We weren't going to go out and blow anybody away, which meant every game would come down to one or two key plays."

The progress made was in attitude . . . the Vikings overcame the futility that had marked the 1984 season without Grant.

"We went into every game believing we could win," said Grant. "We knew it wouldn't be easy, but we knew we would have an opportunity. A chance is all you can ask. Having a chance made the season exciting."

Against the Rams at Anaheim, Derrin Nelson's fourth-down plunge was stopped scant inches short of the goal line with seconds remaining. The Rams won 13–10.

Why, Grant was asked, had he not gone for the point-blank field goal and a tie on fourth down, rather than the touchdown?

"You've got a chance to win the game on one play," Grant responded. "If we went to overtime, anything could happen."

The next week, at Milwaukee, in a situation of eerie similarity, the Vikings faced fourth down at the Packer 1-yard line with less than 2 minutes left in the game. Grant went for the field goal to tie the score at 17 with 1:17 remaining.

But the Packers came back for a field goal of their own to win 20–17.

"The situation was different than in the Rams game," Grant said afterwards. "I didn't feel we had a play that would work there." Pressed to explain further, Grant said, "You'll just have to accept what I said."

Accepting what he said was a sticking point for many as the 1985 season unspooled.

Grant's answers to questions were too simplistic to make the savants comfortable. How could the truth be so uncluttered?

Can be, if it's coming from Grant.

As Grant and his staff labored to restore the team to respectability on the field, ownership factions squared off in a public tug-of-war for control of the franchise.

The Lynn and Winter camps were perceived as warring at the expense of the team on the field.

Did the battle for ownership control serve as a distraction?

"Absolutely not," said Grant.

"That went on in the carpet section," said Bud, using an old, in-house descriptive on separation of the team's executive and coaching ends. The coaching end, to complete the equation, is known as "linoleum."

"What I knew about the situation was what I read in the newspapers," said Grant. "Mike never commented on it, and the only thing Max ever said to me was 'Just go about your business.'

"Max and Mike both have treated me exceptionally well," said Grant. "I consider both of them to be good friends of mine. You have to understand," Grant added, "the whole thing was turned over to the lawyers . . . it wasn't something that involved us. It's like the club dealing with an agent when a player is signed . . . the contact isn't with the player, it's with the agent."

The ownership joust may not have intruded upon Bud's routine, but a mid-year collision with local media did.

The Vikings, at the demand of the NFL office in New York, were required to open the team locker room to reporters on a more frequent basis than just for the traditional post-game interviews. That demand had been originated by local editors.

Grant's response, if not popular with the media, was at least consistent.

"I don't like to be strong-armed by people in high places," he explained.

"The issue was forced upon us," said Grant. "I said, fine, let's look at our entire policy of dealing with the media."

If Grant would be forced to open the locker room to reporters during the week, he would curtail activities in the post-game locker room . . . specifically, he would not permit television crews into the locker room for post-game interviews.

"We put them in a separate room . . . I went in first and did what they wanted from me, and then we brought in players they requested for interviews."

Out of spite?

To an extent, no doubt . . . Grant isn't kidding when he says he doesn't like to be strong-armed.

He also is of an age and tradition to rail stoutly against the admission of women to a football team's post-game locker room.

"I didn't feel we were obliged to open the doors to any women the TV stations decided to send along," he said. "And I'm not the only one who felt that way . . . we had players who objected vehemently to having women in the locker room."

Exiling the post-game cameras wasn't the end of it . . . when reporters were to be admitted to the locker room on a regular basis, Grant declared that assistant coaches would not be available for interviews at any time . . . a "gag" rule.

"It probably was," Grant admitted. "But I also don't feel it's unreasonable to want the players to have the privacy of the locker room. I understand what a reporter wants in the locker room . . . he wants to be able to hear what's being said and generate story angles. I can appreciate that . . . it's a long season, and I'm sure they get tapped out. That's why I tried to come up with something every day. Better that than gossip."

Grant dismissed the dressing room saga as not being a big deal. And to him, no doubt, it wasn't. That it was a big deal to the media is insightful of the game's changing face. It is not a face Grant would be comfortable wearing, any more than a mountain man would be comfortable exchanging his bearskin for a dandy's frockcoat.

If Grant took a certain pleasure from the 1985 season, it was in the effort made by the players.

"They worked hard . . . they worked hard until the last play of the last game. We weren't a strong team to begin with, and then we lost Walker Lee Ashley, a linebacker who is our Singletary [Chicago Bears defensive leader Mike Singletary] , and Jim Hough, who probably was our best offensive lineman."

The final game of the season, a 37–35 loss to Philadelphia at home, exemplified the many near-misses.

"We hit a pass to their 16-yard line and got out of bounds," said Grant. "It was close . . . there might have been one second left, or there might not have been. But the clock showed zero. The script was all there for [Jan] Stenerud . . . a last-second field goal to win the last game of his career. We had the script, but we didn't have the second."

Stenerud, the effervescent Norwegian who was in his nineteenth year as a pro kicker, was a Pro Bowl choice in 1984, but fell on a few hard times in '85.

His missed extra point at Atlanta loomed large as the Vikings lost 14–13. At Green Bay, in the 20–17 defeat, he hit the uprights with two of his three field goal attempts.

Grant on Stenerud.

"He is a class act . . . nobody felt worse than Jan on those misses. He's charted his kicks all the way through . . . after the game against the Packers he told me he had hit the upright only three times in his career. Two of them came in that game."

"As a player," Stenerud said, "you couldn't have a coach you wanted to do well for more than Bud. He's so great in his dealings with the players . . . it gives you a terrible feeling if you don't come through for him."

The Vikings season ended on December 22nd.

Grant outlined his post-season routine during the week leading up to that final game.

"Monday, I'll come in and do the paperwork to tie off the season. Tuesday, I'll go Christmas shopping. Wednesday, we'll have all our family over for Christmas."

And Thursday, he would drive to the Simms Lake retreat. He

didn't say so at the time, but he would go there to ponder his future.

Bud drove back to the Viking offices in Eden Prairie on Saturday. When he had signed his new contract before the 1985 season, it had included a clause giving him the right to notify the club within seven days of the conclusion of a season on whether or not he wished to continue as coach.

"I told Mike I thought it was time for him to find another coach," said Grant.

Why?

Grant laughed.

"The reasons I gave are real reasons," he said. "But a lot of people had trouble accepting them. Nothing had changed . . . the same things that were important to me when I left after the 1983 season were still there. I'm fifty-eight years old, and I've been in professional sports for thirty-six of those years. I decided it was time to enjoy the fruits of those years."

Lynn, once again, suggested that Grant rethink his position.

"We talked throughout that next week," Bud noted. "And it would be incorrect to say I closed the door. We discussed possibilities that would have kept me in the job, we also talked about the direction the club might take without me."

The more they talked, Grant said, the more he came to believe that Lynn's direction, should Bud step down, would be to replace him with Jerry Burns, offensive coordinator and assistant head coach.

But first, Lynn made his effort to keep Grant in the job.

"Sometimes, it's hard for people who deal with money to understand that everything can't be bought," Grant said. "I don't mean money is a god to Mike, or anything like that, but he deals with it all the time, and a lot of that dealing is negotiation. In his job, you work under the assumption that, somewhere, there's a price for everyone. I think it was difficult for Mike to realize there wasn't a sum of money that would matter. I suppose if I had gone to most people and told them what he proposed, they'd say you're crazy if you don't take it. And if I needed things"—and Grant emphasized the word—"then I suppose I would be crazy. But how much money do you need? I have what I believe to be important for myself and my family. I don't need a yacht tied up in Miami . . . if I did, I'd have been beating on his door. But I don't, so I didn't."

Grant explained what he saw as the need to go through the week of negotiating with Mike Lynn.

"I'm going to be here," Grant said. "It was important to me that I treat Mike's job with respect. His job was to show me how I could stay on, but most important, his job was to do what he saw as being the best thing for the club. It was important that Mike feel he had done everything he could from the standpoint of the club."

It has been suggested that Grant insisted on Burns as his replacement.

Insisting isn't Grant's way.

"If you discuss something long enough," he said, "a thing can come around to where it's the other person's idea, but it's what you want done. I didn't try to dictate my thinking to Mike . . . and I really do believe he was thinking beyond our conversations to where hiring Jerry was a logical next step.

"That was when I felt the slate was wiped clean, as far as I was concerned."

Grant had a guilty conscience over his previous resignation for the roles it brought to his veteran assistants.

"When I knew Jerry would get the job, I knew the staff would remain in place," he said. "That was important to me."

But why did he quit . . . really?

Grant shrugged.

"I've read where I quit because my knee's going bad and I don't have many years of mobility left. I played racquetball this morning and I hunted pheasants two weeks ago.

"I read where the real reason I quit was because we have several players who experienced problems with drugs, and young players who held out because of contract disputes. Those things are part of the job . . . if you don't expect to have to deal with them, you're in the wrong business. You don't get paid for making the Xs and Os on the blackboard, you get paid for dealing with the pile of crap you find on your desk every morning. You have to deal with the crap."

Early in the year, one of the issues to be dealt with was developed by Grant himself.

The Vikings were to host Chicago in week three, Thursday night, in a nationally televised game.

The day before the game, Grant let it be known that he thought ABC-TV's practice of not showing the National Anthem on live television was in poor taste.

"After all," he pointed out, "they are called the American Broadcasting Company."

ABC seethed. NFL plenipotentiaries negotiated behind the scenes. Mike Ditka, coach of the visiting Bears, charged his squad with showing stock-still, hand-on-heart respect for the flag during the playing of the anthem. And Grant wondered out loud about having his players sing our patriotic standard on their own once the telecast had begun.

"I believe in the National Anthem," said Grant. "It's important to me. I think it's the highlight of the game."

ABC didn't do the anthem live at the top of its show, but the local ABC affiliate did . . . and the network showed it at halftime.

Call it a draw . . . Grant made what he believed to be a valid point.

"The real reason I resigned again was because I wanted to get on with the other things that are important in my life," said Grant. "Unfortunately, real reasons don't make good copy, so people are going to question them.

"I left the Vikings once and returned to them because they asked me to. Maybe, it was because I felt I owed something to the club. If I did, I feel like I've repaid it."

And what will you do, Bud Grant . . . retiree?

"It surprises me when I say I'm fifty-eight years old. I don't feel old, I don't feel like there's anything I can't do, or any restrictions on me.

"I know what I won't do . . . I won't sit around and grow old. Retirement, for a lot of people, means Sun City or somewhere in Florida. I'm not interested in that. I don't like to be entertained. I have very little desire to watch television or go to movies or read books. My entertainment comes from doing things."

Within the period of roughly one year, Bud Grant went from retiree to active coach to retiree.

Might some people think such a record erratic?

"I wouldn't," said Grant.

Writing in *USA Today* at the time of Grant's final retirement, Gordon Forbes noted:

> He will surely be the next coach in the Pro Football Hall of Fame in Canton. The directors should be forewarned about mice under the tablecloths and salamanders on the dais.

Bud Grant would never admit it, of course, but he couldn't want for a better epitaph to his career, or his life.

Unless it would be the words of a man named Lao-tzu, who lived 565 years before the birth of Christ.

Years ago, Grant read the words in a newspaper. He clipped them out, and they have remained on his desk to this day.

These are the words of Lao-tzu:

> A leader is best when people barely know he exists.
> Not so good, when people obey him and acclaim him.
> Worse, when they despise him.
> But of a good leader who talks little, when his work is done,
> his aim fulfilled, they say:
> 'We did it ourselves.'